JANINE,

YOU KEEP ME [...]

AND LOOKING FORWARD

TO COMING TO THE OFFICE!

TESTIMONIALS

Dwayne Rae has taken an extraordinary set of life experiences and crafted remarkable stories to illustrate the influence we can have on others. His masterfully delivered experiences create an incredible emotional and cognitive impact on each and every listener. Listen closely to his message—you will come away a person changed for the better.

Bishop Decker
Retired HES Manager—Chevron
Leadership Consultant—Global International, Inc.

I first met Dwayne in 2008 and have had the benefit of working with him routinely throughout the years after that. He has always shown a passion for coaching people to come along on the journey of self-awareness for getting everyone home safe each and every day.

But more importantly he delivers his message in a personal and empathetic way. In doing so, I have seen people change their attitudes of 'no change is a good thing' to one where 'I will change for my family, my friends, my colleagues and myself'. And it doesn't make any difference if they are a CEO, a pipefitter, a geologist, a floor worker amongst many different levels of leadership. We have seen them change after hearing his story and why he does what he does.

Be careful though, in reading his story and insights; prepare yourself to make a change in your life, and a change that will challenge a number of your beliefs in a positive way.

Bruce Tarbet
President—JBCC Consulting, Inc.

Dwayne Rae is a dynamic facilitator and speaker who has the ability to break down barriers through his capacity to engage not only the audience as a whole but to engage each individual within the group. The life experiences that Dwayne shares builds laughter and tears as audience members find themselves engrossed in his stories, which are told to exemplify his life learnings.

As you read this book and the arduous life journey that Dwayne has endured, it will become obvious to the reader that Dwayne's passion encompassing safety and leadership comes from the heart along with his intent to help whoever he can along their journeys.

Shane Elder
President—Elder Educational and Consulting Ltd.

Two years ago while working as the Quality Assurance Manager for an organization which provides leadership training across the world, I was introduced to Dwayne as he began his journey to deliver his experience to others. I knew within a couple of days that there was a deep passion in this individual, a sense of commitment to succeed in sharing something with others, but yet I did not know what.

Over the next two years working with Dwayne, listening to his life experience, and seeing the transformation he made within himself and the changes he influenced in others; I went from a coach/mentor in some areas to a student and friend in many other areas. Dwayne turned out to be that "Diamond in the Rough" we have all heard of but rarely get to see in full brilliance.

I wish to thank him for this and congratulate him for the message he has learned to share so well with others to help keep and those around them safe. It is definitely something everyone should read, listen to, and learn from.

David Knight, B.A., B.Ed., CCrm
Safety Consultant

Throughout industry there is a rising group of professionals who incorporate research into business models around leadership, management of change, and the development of a wide variety of management systems.

Dwayne Rae is one such pundit who speaks to groups around the world, delivering passionate messages which incorporate many of these business models into the management of occupational health and safety. What sets Dwayne apart from the pack is his passionate delivery of his personal journey to business leadership. This journey is one of personal suffering and loss which no amount of research could replicate.

Dwayne has overcome these many tragedies and incorporated the most difficult of life lessons into a program which can be shared by all walks of life in both business and personal growth. This story is second only to the passion Dwayne exudes while he delivers this painful but most necessary message.

Turning such adversity to passion in and of itself can be a painful journey, one which Dwayne has harnessed selflessly to inspire and motivate leaders of industry around the world. He not only incorporates his personal story with cutting edge business research and behavioural science but delivers this message with genuine care and concern for others.

It is this passion to systematically improve the lives of others which makes this story a must read for any person who plays a role in influencing the behaviours of others professionally or personally.

Murray Ritchie, MSc, CHSC, CMIOSH
Managing Director—Tri-Lens Consulting

Dwayne Rae is, quite simply, an impressive and captivating young man.

I first met him several years ago when he was preparing to co-facilitate (for the first time) a three-day Health & Safety Leadership Workshop with another Leadership Professional and myself.

My initial impression was of a very physically fit, serious, and focused young man. On the first day, as he delivered his assigned material, I was a little concerned that his seriousness and imposing physique might be a little unsettling for our leader participants. I was thinking, "Who is this cocky and impatient young Turk?"

However, as the workshop progressed and he warmed to his subject, he started to relax. We observed a solid understanding and knowledge about leadership and its many pitfalls, beginning to surface. Additionally, we saw the glimmer of a wonderful sense of humor and playfulness emerging. I started to think, "This young man has great potential." ... Little did I realize!

When Dwayne shares the "ups and downs" of his personal and professional experiences it is obvious he has had a journey in both life and leadership that not many can compare. What also soon became apparent was his innate intelligence, incredible memory and remarkable intuitive skills. When you add his excellent public speaking skills to this combination, you realize he is the "whole package"!

Since then, we have come to know each other very well. My respect for him, both professionally and personally, has grown significantly. Although twenty years separate us, I regard him as a true friend and colleague.

Through his dedication to observing, studying, and striving to better understand the qualities of a good leader I have seen him rapidly evolve into one himself. He constantly strives to exhibit those qualities in all aspects of his life, and it shows.

Simply put, if you haven't read his book—do so, it is well worth it. If you have an opportunity to hear him speak, take it; you will not regret it!

Alan K. McDonald, CRSP
Managing Director & Leadership Consultant—Pulse-8 Safety
Consultants Inc.
Calgary, Alberta Canada

"Dynamically Captivating," "Informative," "Motivating," and "Inspiring" are just a few of the comments we have received from our workforce in regards to the Global International Program, "Safety Essentials for Managers and Supervisors." Combined with the knowledge and skill of Dwayne Rae to effectively, educate, coach, and mentor our Leaders has truly made a difference within our safety performance and culture today. His passion, desire, personal experiences, and stories shared throughout the SEFSAM Program, has without a doubt had a positive impact on our leaders.

He has not only challenged, he has inspired our leaders with new ideas and approaches on how to motivate our workforce and how to create a culture that values safety at home, at work, and as a way of life.

On behalf of the Noel team, we would like to recognize and thank Dwayne for the outstanding, influential, and impactful role he has had on our workforce and our corporation as a whole. Dwayne's dedication, genuine character, and "can do" attitude have helped our leaders to transfer newly gained skills and understandings into success!

I recommend everyone to read this book, share it with others and watch the change in our own behaviours through Dwayne's life stories.

Don Hicks
BP Major Projects Construction Superintendent

Prior to first meeting Dwayne, I had no preconceptions or background. He was "just another guy" spreading the word. However, from the first moment, his personal passion and commitment was obvious. After hearing the tragic details of the life changing events he has captured in his writings, I realized this man "needed" to get out and share the message with as many people as possible to help prevent "them" from living a nightmare that never ends.

Dwayne has the ability to connect with his audience almost instantly. His personal presence and charisma, coupled with sharing the tragic events as they unfolded, are profoundly powerful. This power drives dramatic personal safety commitment shifts in his audiences rarely seen.

Glenn Morasch-President
Top Flyte Safety Consultants

Over the course of the past 2.5 years I've had the pleasure to work closely with Dwayne Rae. Dwayne is a colleague who has some very compelling reasons to renew your focus on personal leadership and safety. Dwayne shares a powerful message on this topic about heartfelt personal loss from shortcomings in this arena.

He delivers his message in a fashion that is both entertaining yet hard hitting that takes you on a journey through many emotions from laughter to tears of sorrow. I feel fortunate to have the opportunity to know Dwayne and have him share these experiences of his real life on a very personal level with me. His life story is a compelling one that will captivate you and leave you pondering your own personal safety.

J. Gary Carnduff
President—1236696 Alberta Ltd
Global International Consultant

What If:

A Lifetime's Reflection on Safety and Leadership

Dwayne Rae

authorHOUSE®

AuthorHouse™
1663 Liberty Drive
Bloomington, IN 47403
www.authorhouse.com
Phone: 1-800-839-8640

First published by AuthorHouse 1/4/2011

ISBN: 978-1-4567-1799-5 (sc)
ISBN: 978-1-4567-1797-1 (e)
ISBN: 978-1-4567-1798-8 (hc)

Library of Congress Control Number: 2010919595

Printed in the United States of America

For those who believed in me ...
before I believed in myself.

Introduction

I grew up in a small town called Prince Rupert—a beautiful city that has seen its share of hard times since I was born there in 1971, Prince Rupert is a coastal community on British Columbia's border with Alaska. Beautiful mountain ranges, lakes, rivers, and rain. That's right, rain.

Prince Rupert is famous for two things—world class salmon fishing and rain. We like to say it only rains twice a year ... once from March until about October and then from October until about March.

The Prince Rupert I knew growing up was a small city of hard working people, people who worked in canneries, sawmills, pulp mills, in the thriving local fishing industry, and in various logging camps full of forestry workers.

So much has changed in the sleepy little city since I was young. The fishing industry has come onto hard times. The local pulp mill—which once employed several hundred people directly, and several thousands indirectly—has been closed for a decade. Along with that closing came the shutting down of several large and small timber mills and the evaporation of an entire forest industry.

The little town that seemed so prosperous when I was growing up has certainly seen better days.

I bring up Prince Rupert because it is where this story both starts and finishes ... and then starts again. I am long removed from my days in Prince Rupert when I worked in the forest industry. I travel the world these days as a leadership facilitator, working for an organization dedicated to changing lives around the globe.

I have the great pleasure to work with executives and senior managers from various industries on how to create the "want to" in a workforce to work safely. I speak on motivation, communication, risk management, and managing performance issues each week. I have spoken to groups from Anchorage, Alaska to Halifax, Nova Scotia; Cincinnati, Ohio to Houston, Texas; and just recently Luanda, Angola in Africa.

I work with the Global Training Leadership group out of Calgary, and each week we speak all over the world on the necessity of empowering our workforce with the motivation to make the right decisions in any and all work places.

The irony is that I made decisions years ago, over fifteen years ago to be exact, that were based on how to make more money or increase production. This meant that I was eroding one of the four cornerstones of business ... safety.

This book tells why I made those decisions. I hope my story moves you in a way so that you don't ever have to find out the way I did about what happens when you make the wrong decisions. Even if you think they are the right decisions when you make them.

My heart went into this book in a way that was very painful. It was healing in some respects, but ultimately so intensely disturbing that I couldn't sleep properly for the better part of one year. I will not keep the truth from you—I cried every time I began to work on each page, every chapter.

My hope is that no one else ever has to learn the way I did. I hope you will find honesty in my passion and make it part of our journey together to make the workplace safer for everyone.

Dwayne Rae

Chapter One
I Knew This Was
Going to Happen

Have you ever been sitting around after an accident and had someone look at you and say, "I knew this was going to happen"?

A grieving widow on February 14, 1995 made that very comment to me as I sat with her at her kitchen table. She was gazing into space, not focused on anything, but I knew there was something she was picturing in her mind. She looked tired. The truth was, she was exhausted. She had not slept for two days. Her hair was dishevelled, her eyes puffy and red, her arms were crossed over her body, and she was holding herself as children often do when in pain or fearful. There was a reason why this woman was in this state.

Two days before, on February 12, I met this woman at the top of the stairs in her home after I had spent the entire day looking for her husband in the cold and dark waters of the Pacific Northwest. We never did find his body; he was missing and presumed drowned. This was a wife's worst fear, a mother's terror, the love of her life … gone.

When I met her at the top of the stairs in her home I never did say the words, "He is dead." I just couldn't say it. Those words are too unnatural. I tried to speak, but I couldn't. I just vainly tried to choke back tears and she knew.

As I stood in front of this woman, her world falling apart, I put my arms up beside my head and clasped tightly around my ears, trembling. I couldn't speak. She looked at me, and as redness overtook the whites of her eyes she began to shake. Her voice weak and crackling, she asked in an almost-whisper, "Where is he, Dwayne?" Then she collapsed into my arms, crying.

When I stood at the top of her stairs, I saw a pain that was not explainable. It was incomprehensible. As you read through these pages and follow this terrible journey, I deplore you to "always do what needs to be done" to ensure you never experience these situations in your life. My hope is no one *ever* finds themselves responsible and forever guilty knowing that a life has been lost.

I had to stare into the eyes of a crying wife and mother of three boys. Those eyes waken me far too often and I relive that day every day since it happened. I was witness to a family that came unravelled, and where there was so much love before, there was for a time only confusion and hurt and pain.

Let me walk you through a tragedy that I had to witness. It is actually a bunch of tragedies all rolled into one. They all play into each other and if it not for one, none of the others would have occurred or ever made sense.

I ask myself often, "What if?"

Chapter Two
Where it All Started

I began working for a small, family-run logging company on a part-time basis back in 1986. The company owner, Norman, lived in my neighborhood, so one night my friends and I played street hockey in front of his house until he came home from work that night. Summer was still four months away, but other boys in the neighborhood had worked for Norman during the summer and I wanted to get to him before anyone else.

I asked if I could work for him during the school break, and he told me that if my parents said it was okay, he would give me some work so I could buy a car when I turned sixteen. It must have looked pretty funny to him, because if my memory serves me true, I think I asked him for a summer job while I was holding my hockey stick in my hands.

I would be fifteen years old that summer. Like any teenager at that age, I thought I had the answers to all of life's challenges. In reality, of course, I knew pretty much nothing, but there was no way you could tell me that back then. As a parent today, I am nodding my head as I write this, and maybe chuckling a little bit, too, as I am starting to see this behavior in my own children. I was typical of any teenage boy at that age. I was consumed by thoughts of cars and girls and school. I am kidding, of course. I never thought about school.

My plan was to work that summer and the next to save some money to buy a car as I turned sixteen (about a year away) so I could get to school. No, that's not true. I wanted the car so I could get girls.

In truth, I needed the car. I was an ugly child raised by even uglier parents. The only way I was going to get a date back in 1986 was if I had the car, or so I thought. Turns out that most teenage girls were much more mature than the teenage boys my age, and those girls I was trying to impress were more interested in the eighteen-year-old young men with cars than the sixteen-year-old boy.

I went to ask my mom and dad if I could go to work at Norman's log yard about four months before summer, and my parents looked shocked. My mom asked, "Why there?" My response was based on money. A log yard meant about ten bucks an hour—a tidy sum for a kid in 1986.

I remember vividly that my mom looked nervous about this, so I looked to Dad for support. In my family it was Mom who ran the household. Dad was involved, which meant agreeing with mom when required, but mom ran the household. So when I looked to Dad for support he didn't say much.

Dad actually said something a little out of the ordinary to my mom. "Let's go chat about this for a minute alone," he said. Mom agreed, and I sat and waited at the kitchen table for about fifteen minutes. They came back and had an idea to share. They told me I could work at Norman's log yard as long as I worked at the local McDonald's beforehand for at least three months. The look on my face must have been priceless.

Nothing against McDonald's, but that wasn't where I saw my career starting, I mean those McDonald's uniforms were sexy back in 1986, but I just couldn't see this as something that would work for me.

I remember asking, "Why McDonald's?" They told me that McDonald's has a system of training their employees where an order is given verbally and the worker must repeat that instruction back word for word.

Here's an example. "Dwayne, I need two Big Macs and three Quarter Pounders with cheese."

I then repeat back to the crew lead, "Yes, two Big Macs and three Quarter Pounders with cheese."

Then the crew boss acknowledges again with a "yes" or a "no."

Simple, right? It provides for a perfect understanding of the required task. From what I am told, this is how the military works. It does lead to effective workplace communication. This is why mom and dad wanted me to work at McDonald's first. They believed (and rightly so) that I needed to understand the importance of communication prior to starting any work.

Even though they presented a sound argument for the clear communication I would need in the workplace, I remember at the time thinking, "They just don't think I will work at McDonald's and this is their way of saying no without actually to saying it."

I must admit that I wasn't too keen on this idea back then. McDonald's wasn't the cool place to work. I had to convince my friends that working there would be cool so I wouldn't be made of fun. If I remember this right, I convinced my two closest friends to sign up with me and we went to work for McDonald's.

The deal with mom and dad was pretty simple. Work at McDonald's for three months and then I could go to work for the log yard. When mom and dad put this stipulation into place, I am positive they figured that if I worked at McDonald's for a time that I would drop my desire to work at the log yard and I would then be working in a safer climate. So, imagine their surprise when I came home after day ninety-one and proclaimed that I had quit.

Mom and Dad were not happy. They sat me down at the kitchen table and I got the talk about responsibility and commitment and blah blah blah. I had to remind them that they made the deal with me and I lived up to my end. There was further talk about those things already mentioned, but we had an agreement, so they had to grin and bear it. I was going to work at the log yard in about two weeks, making ten bucks and hour compared to $2.65 at McDonald's.

I must thank the McDonald's organization, though. Throughout my working career I have repeated instructions given to me and I have to tell you, their training works.

So there I was after my McDonald's stint, starting my real working career. I still remember the first day. Mom made me a pretty bag lunch and had all my former play clothes laid out for me. I was a working man (boy) now. Just the night before I played street hockey for three hours and scored nine goals in a game that ended up being a real tight affair at twenty-eight to twenty-five. I was a local hero that night. I scored a couple of goals just before 10 p.m. when we all had to go home for the night. Hey, I was only fifteen, and 10 p.m. was late back in my neighborhood in 1986.

I got picked up by three guys who occupied the front seat of the pickup, so I had to sit in the back of the truck. It was 7 a.m.. Nothing troubling for me, though, as I was one of those kids who used to really impress his parents by waking up at 5:30 a.m. all the time and figuring they must want to be up, too.

Norman had been in the loop on my McDonald's requirement and gave me instructions the day before on where to be and who would pick me up. He kept reminding me *not* to be late.

We drove the fifteen minutes out of town to the log sort yard that I was going to work at for my two-month summer break. Most of my friends didn't want to work that summer. They still had the one last chance to hang out and I was bucking the trend, but I wanted that car. The log yard where I spent my first summer working for Norman was where he brought all his harvested logs for sorting. The logs were brought in two ways.

The first and most common method was by water. The log sort yard was in a bay on the water. A large body of water that was accessible during high tides by the marine system. Large log booms were put together miles away at one of Norman's operations and these large log booms were towed to this log yard by large tug boats. The wood was then separated from the log bundles and moved up to the log yard where each log was scaled by professional log scalers who graded and recorded the meterage, which helps set the wood value.

After being scaled, the wood received a mark or grade and then grades of wood were re-bundled together and dropped back into the water on the other side of the log yard.

The other method of bringing harvested timber into the log yard was by logging truck. Several logging trucks would show up during the day from another logging block that Norman operated about twenty-five kilometers (about fifteen miles) outside of town. No matter how the logs showed up at the log yard, it was a terribly busy place.

I remember unloading my gear and almost no one gave me the time of day. I just stood by the truck not knowing what to do while everyone began to go and fire up huge log loaders, D7 cats, chainsaws, and compressors. I was in awe of all the equipment. I was wondering what big and beautiful piece of equipment I would be operating for the summer when I was introduced (sort of) to a man named Charlie. I saw Charlie coming toward me, and as he walked awkwardly toward me I remember thinking he could quite possibly be the ugliest man on the planet. Ever judge a book by its cover? I did this day. Charlie was going to give me some things to think about.

Chapter Three
My Time with Charlie

Charlie was an older guy. He was my boss for the summer, and he came over and asked if I was going to stand around all day or actually get working. I remember his smile was wrong. By wrong, I mean he was missing most of his teeth. His face drooped on one side and he had patches of hair growing on his head. When he asked me if I was going to stand around all day, it took everything I had to not start laughing at all the teeth he didn't have.

My parents raised me to be polite and respectful and answer questions with well-thought-out answers. So when Charlie asked me if I was going to work or not, I came up with this well thought out response, "Huh?"

He did not look amused, and his one eye lifted strangely. That was when I noticed that his eyes did not seem to focus on one point. One eye would be looking straight at me and the other looked off in a different direction. Which eye should I look at?

He repeated what I had just said to him. "Huh? Are you some kind of smart ass?" he asked.

I then thought about the correct answer. Logic for logic was how my parents raised me. I came up with, "Well, if you think that 'huh' was a smart answer, then we're all in trouble." I sat back in the glow of a good response, or so I thought. I gave a little nervous chuckle at the end of my statement to show I was trying to be humorous as well as logical. This is where a fifteen year old gets treated like a fifteen-year-old smart ass and a fifty-year-old veteran has his fun.

Charlie looked at me and said, "Kid, let's get something straight. I

9

see one or two of you summer kids every year and you know how many times they quit before summer is out"?

I thought about it. He was working my logic against me. I realized that by the way he was asking this question that the answer is all of them quit, otherwise he wouldn't have asked it. So I answer back with, "All of them."

He smiled coldly, still missing half his teeth, and said, "Wrong, none. Because they understand I am here to help them and I keep their interests at heart." He looked at me with a cruel smile, and as a tooth fell out, he said, "I am willing to make you the first that doesn't make it."

The son of a gun outflanked me. His logic was better than mine. I was going to have to talk with mom and dad. What a bunch of crap. What Charlie was trying to teach me was that my keys to making it safely through the summer rested in his hands, and if I was going to screw around it was going to be a short summer working for me. He would rather let me go than deal with a smart-ass kid who really knew nothing. It was work safe or don't work for ten-teeth Charlie.

Lesson learned. Charlie, one. Dwayne, zero.

So I begrudgingly lowered my head, said I was sorry, and began learning from Charlie and the others in the worksite about how to stay out of trouble. "Don't put your hands here," was something I must have heard a couple hundred times in the first week. There was no grey, it was black and white. It was do it the right way or you won't be here. Stay away from this equipment, don't touch that, wear your gloves, wear your hard hat, and so on and so on. It all came back to, "don't put your hands here," it seemed.

What was funny about this common statement was that almost everyone I saw was at some point doing exactly what I was told not to do. "Don't put your hands in the pinch on the crimping pot." The crimping pot was like an air pot that had jaws on it that could apply a tremendous amount of force to pinch closed an aluminum crimp onto two wires in a wood rack that assured when the wood was dumped into the water that all the logs stayed together in a bundle. So how come they were allowed to put their hands in places I wasn't? What was the difference?

They had been around a lot longer, and they all seemed to violate the rules. They told me *not* to do something and then went out and did it. How come the double standard? This actually started to bother me after about the tenth day. So I thought I should challenge someone about this and then I could be one of the boys, even though they were all men and I was the only boy.

During lunch on day ten I ask a guy named Tom why he put his hands inside the crimping jaws. He looked at me disgustingly and offered this gem. "Why are you asking, know nothing?" I explained that I was told not to do that and I wondered why he was. He looked unimpressed and said, "Because I can." He then turned toward the other men on the crew and imitated me asking my stupid question. Well, at least I entertained them over lunch. I was embarrassed. I wanted to honestly know *why* he was doing it … I guess the way I asked the question wasn't to his liking. And I paid for it by having everyone laugh at me for not knowing.

I went home that night and told my parents what had happened and that I did not want to go back to work the next day. My dad looked concerned and my mom said, "I thought you were too young to be there, anyway." My dad didn't say too much until he had me alone after dinner. He asked a few more questions about the day and why I asked Tom the question.

I explained to my dad that I was told not to do something, and then the guys did just what they told me not to do. I was getting mixed messages. I was told one thing and witnessed another. When I did follow the rules, the guys made fun of me. They would tap me on my hard hat and say things like, "There's nothing to protect in here" and laugh cruelly. When I wore a high-visibility vest they said, "We put that vest on you so we can always know where stupid is."

I had no idea what could or couldn't hurt me. Sure, there were things that seemed obvious, like not running under heavy moving equipment or touching a chainsaw blade while the saw was on. But there were so many things that were not obvious. All anyone ever talked about was using "common sense." Where did common sense come from? I remember that it made me sick that guys would tease me about wearing gloves while working.

The guys would say things like, "rookies wear gloves," and "green horns need gloves to protect their pinkies," and the guys would have a good laugh. The part that made me sick was these stupid jack assess were all missing fingers. These idiots would make fun of me for trying to work safe and then brag about losing a finger. I would even challenge one or two of them when they were pushing me too much and the best comment of all came from Tom, who made fun of me more than anyone.

His response to losing the tip of his finger was, "You're not a man until you lose a finger."

He had lost half a finger months before in an incident. Did that mean he was half a man? I asked him that at lunch one day when he was making more fun of me than usual. It went over real well. Here was a steroid-ingesting moron getting outsmarted by a fifteen year old.

As you can imagine, the abuse continued from him. That night my dad and I talked, and I teared up. I wanted to fit in, but I wanted to fit in working safely. Dad told me quitting would be worse for me. He was right, of course. I was scared, though. I really didn't know what I was doing. Dad wanted me to be safe, but did I really know what safe was?

Chapter Four
My Lesson as a Young Fella

I got through that first summer. I made a lot of money compared to my slack-ass friends and eventually I did earn the respect of many of the guys I worked with. Not all, but most. That fella Tom, he and I ended working around each other on and off. We never did see eye to eye. I'll explain more later.

That first summer I made the money and unexpectedly bought a car. I originally thought I would work two summers and save up money for a car, but while I was still fifteen (a full year before I could apply for a learner's permit), my dad helped me negotiate the purchase of a 1975 Triumph TR-6 sports car. What a beauty. It was a good thing I made good money that summer because I bought the car for two thousand dollars and then my dad helped me spend another four thousand dollars on new fenders, a new roof, and a new red paint job. Every time I said, "Dad, I'm not sure if I'm going to have all the money," he would just smile and say, "Don't you want to do this right?"

Of course, that car was going to help my grades in school. Not really—I was hoping it would help this ugly child with the girls. So I had a car before I could drive—imagine that problem. I needed to work more than one summer to pay for all the improvements I made to the car. By the end of my first working summer, I think I still owed my dad two thousand dollars for work done to the car he had already paid for.

Over the course of the year we got the car fixed up and tuned up. By the tail end of the summer of 1987 the car was all finished. It was a beautiful car. I was beginning to appreciate the comments Dad had been making all year about the car's lines and engineering.

As summer was ending and the car was finished, my dad came to me one afternoon. We were looking over the car, and he commented on how good it looked. After the latest tune up, the engine purred, something I didn't really appreciate back then. My big concern was how the seats folded down. I was planning to get a little action, after all. Dad said, "Let's take 'er for a rip." He had a huge smile on his face as he ran his eyes across the car. I got into the passenger seat and handed him the keys and he looked at me smiling and said, "This is your car, son, you drive."

Dad and I cruised out to a road just outside of town that went to a local coal terminal. It was a long, flat road with very little traffic. As we hit the road, my dad told me to punch it. I was puzzled. When I got my driver's license just three months before, Dad told me never to speed, and if he caught me he'd take the car away. Now he was telling me to speed up. I looked at him again and he said, "Let's see what this car can do."

This must be a set-up, I thought. I refused and asked, "Why?"

He smiled back and said, "Trust me. I want to do this with you. Open her up, Dwayne." That was good enough for me. Within fifteen seconds I got that little sports car up to about 110 miles an hour. Dad was sitting next to me with a grin and I was smiling like never before. Then he said, "Okay. Pull it over at the end of the road at the turnout." I do as instructed and he said, "Shut the car off, son." As I do he gathered a breath and said, "This car is too fast for you. You are too young to have a car that can go this fast. I have to sell it."

Imagine getting punched in the balls. Remember the first time when you were a teenager and actually had balls? Imagine that feeling, but not just a punch. Imagine someone jumping up and down on them. That is how I felt sitting there. I was stunned. Dad helped me pick this car out. He helped me sand it down, worked with me on making it beautiful. Now he was telling me I must get rid of it.

"Why?" was the only question I could get out of my mouth. I was actually trying not to cry. I felt a lump in my throat build up and I felt a little short of breath. This was my dream car.

Dad took a deep breath and said, "I care about you way too much to let you kill yourself in this car."

As I sat there in stunned silence I thought of a whole bunch of logical things I could say to change his mind. When I thought I had the perfect response crafted for discussion, I looked at my father and saw something in his eyes I had never seen before. I don't know how to explain it, but he had a look of concern I can't describe. Years later I asked him what he was thinking about that gave him that look on his face, and he said he was thinking of me killing myself in that car.

As we were sitting in the car that day I didn't have it in me to challenge him. I already knew his answer wasn't going to change. Dad never changed his mind once it was made unless Mom told him to change it. Even as a teenage punk I knew that the look on his face indicated a concern at a depth I had not seen before and probably would not understand until I had my own children.

This is the ultimate show of concern from a parent. My dad knew his decision was not going to be popular. He cared about that, but he cared more about my safety and my well being, and he wasn't going to be part of my death, No matter what, popular or not.

Years later, when I became a manager for different companies, I took that same approach many times. No matter what, and popular or not, I was not going to allow people to be hurt on my watch. It sounds simple, but it isn't. Not even a little bit.

Trying to explain the rationale behind taking a teenager's car away is similar to telling a worker who has worked a certain way for years to change the way they perform a task when he or she has never had an accident. Many people fail to recognize the need to change if there hasn't been some sort of loss. Why would I change if I have never been hurt?

Working for years without injury doesn't mean that a job or task is not risky. It may mean that the safety filters in place to ensure we have always worked safely are working. Far too often people say things like, "We have always done it that way, so why should we change?" That's a valid argument if the conditions were always perfect and we as humans were always perfect. We are not, and the conditions are usually not perfect, either, so guess what is bound to happen? Loss.

As we drove home together and very little was said, I began to realize that my life was more valuable than the car to dad. I resented him for that for a few months at least. The fact I recall that event so vividly maybe means I was stung by it more than I was willing to admit.

When we arrived home, Dad told Mom that he was selling my car. Mom was very happy. In fact, Dad took my car and traded it in for my mom and gave her a brand new car. I got my mom's used 1984 Ford Tempo. I know, right? Hot car back then. The Ford Tempo was never a hot car. Sorry, Ford.

It was a four door, too. My parents kept saying to me how safe that car was. That my friends would die for a car like that. I told my parents to give it to my friends. Not the answer they wanted to hear.

My parents were happy. I was not. I was unhappy because I didn't really agree with the decision or the rationale or logic behind it. My parents had a world of experience behind their decision making. I was influenced by getting girls and making myself popular with the other kids. Let's face it, not many sixteen year olds have sports cars. Not many sixteen year olds even have cars.

I didn't care about the safety issues. I didn't have the depth or maturity to understand their point of view. Now here's the rub. The same influencers that worked against me at sixteen years old are the same ones that influence people at forty-six years old. No wonder we have so many workplace injuries!

Chapter Five
The Average Worker's Thoughts on Safety

I went back to work for that same logging company the next summer. The second summer went a little smoother than the first. I had the respect of some of the guys. Some not so much. Remember Tom? He and I did not see eye to eye that second summer, either. In fact, our relationship got worse.

An interesting trend developed during that second summer. I began to notice that although every worker on the log yard was told to not do certain things because those things were unsafe, I can recall seeing the same activities over and over again done the way we were all told not to. The real kicker too was that every time someone did an unsafe act and was able to get the job done a little quicker by cutting a corner, he or she got rewarded with praise.

In fact, the only time anyone seemed to get in trouble was when someone tried to cut a corner and then they got hurt. Otherwise, "Great job." I came to this sort of paradigm almost every day in my working career. In fact, as I gained experience and sorted my way through these dangerous situations, I found myself even rolling the dice to "git-r-done."

I used to cut corners by removing certain engineered guards that were in place on several pieces of equipment. The guarding made it difficult in some cases to work fast. Guards, after all, are usually designed to ensure that people can't place body parts into the moving gears or parts. This inability to work around the guards sometimes means that time is gobbled up by only being able to work in a linear fashion.

Think of your garden shed. Most of us use some sort of power tools. We often remove the guarding on a weed whacker because the guard doesn't allow us to cut the weeds close to the fence. Or, my favorite from logging, removing the guard that stops the chainsaw from running once the saw gets to a certain depth into the wood. This guard triggers a switch that shuts down the chainsaw when in a certain position. However, that guard is always removed by loggers because it shuts down the saw far too often.

The "git-r-done" catch phrase sucks. It is the one of the reasons behind so many workplace incidents that it makes me cringe. I had a few incidents along the way because of my complete lack of understanding surrounding the need that must exist to do the task safely, or not at all.

And in so many cases it isn't due to a lack of knowledge or skill. It is due to a lack of wanting to do the right thing. Our culture in the workplace is so backwards. I have seen it time and time again where people will talk a great game surrounding doing things safely and then people will go out and do exactly the opposite that they just said they would never do.

And again, I am a prime example of this throughout my career.

So how do we ensure that everybody works safe so that we don't have losses? Interesting and simple question, right? Think about it. Why do people work at risk?

Simple question. Very complicated answer.

Think of all the different things we deal with on a personal level every day! The stress that daily life brings us, from mortgage payments to car payments to household bills. Okay, those are the easy issues that cause us pretty minor grief. Try this instead. The birth of a child, raising that child, trying to get that child and maybe another one or two children raised without injury or incident and then prepare them for adulthood and university and … holy crap, right?

Now let's take it really deep. Try to balance the household budget, raise our children, keep them safe, try to please our spouse, and then ultimately deal with our parents catching a disease, struggling with their mortgage payment and their life that has now become our life, and oh yeah … I left the best for last. We have a career in the middle of all this that has some pretty major ups and downs as well.

I have yet to meet a person in the workplace who comes up to me and says, "Let's see if I can hurt myself today." We have maybe met people whom we think *must* want to hurt themselves based on their blatant disregard for what many would see as the obvious rules of engagement to ensure safety, but I can't remember meeting someone who went out and willingly tried to harm themselves.

Many of us have come across those individuals who tell us they have hurt themselves, and although there are no witnesses and they cannot recall their incident with any consistency and the injury can't be diagnosed, they still claim to be the safest workers in the world.

So how do we offer ideas about how each of us can begin to work through the scenarios mentioned, and how can we apply certain fundamentals to real situations for a safer workplace?

Let's talk about where safety came from for a little bit.

If you went to average Joe worker in the field and asked, "How long has safety been around?" you most commonly find two trains of thought.

One answer is "forever," and the other is "twenty years, but we got really focused on safety in the last ten years."

Safety has, in fact, been around for thousands of years. You can go back to the time of King Hamurabi of Babylon and find evidence that safety existed. The Hamurabic tablets that were unearthed date back to 2100 bc and those tablets bring ultimate accountability. Eye for an eye stuff. Overseer builds house, house collapses, killing owner, and the builder gets put to death. Eye for an eye.

Now, some people wish things were still that way as it would drive behaviors a little better, but we'll come back to the "getting performance" aspect at the end of the book.

I have mentioned already that I have yet to find people who try to get hurt. Maybe someone else has seen this. I haven't, and I base my findings on what I have been exposed to. So, if no one is consciously going out and trying to hurt themselves, then how come it keeps happening?

My research has indicated that people got rewarded for unsafe behaviors. Please let me explain. As I mentioned from my log yard experience of my first summer, people were out performing tasks in a manner that was unsafe. The only time anyone got in trouble at the log yard was when they got hurt.

Everyone seemed to know their jobs. The work was always there to be done. People would operate equipment, and as long as no one got hurt, we just kept on working. When someone decided it was time to cut a corner and it didn't work out for them, there was trouble. The job would stop, and perhaps someone would administer first aid. We all hoped first aid wasn't necessary, because anytime we needed first aid it meant that a report would filled out, the company owner would be called, and there would be a meeting. In many cases someone lost their job.

So, every time someone cut a corner and they got the task done without injury it was acceptable. In fact, they were usually rewarded with "good job." So let me ask this question. If every time someone cut a corner and got injured and then the result was they got fired or reprimanded, how often were people willing to honestly report any loss?

You know the answer.

It drives the actual reporting underground. When things are driven underground, we don't really get to the real issues onsite. There is still all this cutting the corner stuff going on and we don't really know about it because people hide it. That is dangerous.

This was what I saw over and over and over again. I even remember one day that guy Tom saying that all this safety stuff onsite actually slowed them down from doing the real work. He also said he was going to tell Norman, the company owner, that this safety stuff was crap. I thought this would be an interesting exchange. Tom was a big guy who spent time in the gym, and Norman was a medium-built older guy. I figured Tom would tell him.

Sure enough, we had a meeting one day to discuss some workplace issues, and Tom had his chance. He had been telling everyone for weeks that he would show Norman how it was. Norman got up and talked to everyone, and then he said, "Any questions?" The room fell silent.

Norman then said, "Come on, guys, I need to hear from you." No one really talked about safety. It was all about new equipment and production targets and so on. I was sitting there, staring at Tom, and he was kissing Norm's ass. It was actually embarrassing to watch. If Norm had coughed, he would have to push Tom's tongue out of the way to wipe his nose, because Tom had it so far up Norm's ass.

I was watching Tom, and my respect for him started to slide off. I didn't really have much respect for him anyway, because he was mean to people and he had made fun of me, but this love fest was brutal.

He actually had a point, or so it seemed. Even though I didn't like Tom, a lot of the other guys did, and they agreed with him when he was talking about this safety stuff that slowed them all down. So as I was sitting there I was thinking, "Here is my opportunity to show the guys I have their interests at heart." As Norm was wrapping up the meeting, I took the initiative. I put my hand up and said, "May I offer something I have been hearing the guys talk about?"

I had eight guys all turn their heads and stare at me with fear. I think a few guys stopped breathing. They must have known what was coming.

Chapter Six
Speaking Out

Norm looks at me, smiled, and said, "Of course!" As I looked around the room and I begin to speak, every single set of eyes was on me. I should have stopped right there. I probably shouldn't have even started. I even thought about stopping, but as I looked at Norm's face, I can see that he was eager to hear from me. So I say the following, "The guys have been talking about how we could get a lot more done around here if we had less of this safety stuff to do."

Imagine a bomb going off. Norm's smile turned upside down, and one of his eyes actually lowered and twitched. Think of John Wayne with the squint of death. Norm looked at me. Actually, he looked right through me. This was bad. I could tell by his body language and breathing pattern that he was not entirely pleased with my statement. What's worse, I looked around the room, and everyone was staring at the floor except for Tom. He was staring right at me, wide eyed. As bad as this situation was, I was going to make it worse. I looked at Norman and said, "Tom was just talking this morning and we all agreed that we only get in trouble when we get caught."

Norman's breathing started to return to normal and a grin returned to his face. Calm before the storm? This grin wasn't quite as warm as the smile he had a few minutes ago. This grin almost looked devilish. The rest of room, including Tom, was just staring at the floor. I was only one looking at Norman. He was looking around at all the lowered heads. He was a man who built this company up over his lifetime. His money paid all our wages, he owned every piece of equipment.

A few seconds went by. He walked over to me, shook my hand, and said, "Thank you." I was confused. He asked with a smile and a laugh if anyone else had anything to add. No one lifted their head or answered. He said, "Okay" and walked out. Just before closing the door he asked me to meet him outside.

I was getting fired. I walked out and prepared for the worst. Norman looked at me, smiled, and put his arm over my shoulder. He asked me to walk with him. *Here it comes*, I thought. Instead, he just walked with me, asking how things were going. He told me that Charlie says I work hard and that he appreciated that. He stopped about one hundred feet from the office and started talking.

The whole talk was about how those guys are just like any other guys. He told me they will say they are going tell Norm how it is and so on, but it's all just BS. He explained how guys in a gang mentality will say they are going do this and that, but when it really comes down to it, they won't. As I sat there in the midday sun, I began to realize that this man was correct. In some ways that mentality could be linked to the behaviors we see in high schools, or on worksites.

As I listened to Norm, my thoughts began to turn to the guys who were still in the office just off this log yard, finishing their lunch but probably also getting ready to kill me. I had called them out and thought I was going to gain their respect and had done entirely the opposite. I was dead. I wondered if my parents would ever find my body.

Would anyone miss me? I felt like I was going to throw up, and then Norm brought me back to his attention and told me to wait right and that he'd be right back. He walked back toward the office and went inside. I never knew what he said in there. Whatever it was, it kept me alive, because he came back out with Charlie and they told me that everything was going to be okay.

I thought I was going to cry. The weight of what I did started to really weigh heavy and they must have seen it because they talked very gently to me. Nine-tooth Charlie (that's right nine, not ten, one more had fallen out) was laughing saying things like, "The guys will know better than to mouth off around you now." They both got me calmed down, and guys began to exit the office to go back to work. Some even walked up to me and shared a smile and a laugh and walked on.

Tom came out last. He looked around the yard and then realized where I was. He gave me "the look" and started walking toward me. He came close to me and stared at me with great disgust, then gave me the middle finger and did not talk to me for three more summers. Good, I didn't like him anyway.

As I went about my work for a couple of hours, Norm came back to me and asked me to talk with him for a few minutes. *Here it comes, now I'm getting fired.* Instead of firing me, Norman asked to me share what I saw that scared me. I did not want to admit I was scared, but he just sat there smiling at me, so eventually I shared with him stories about people putting fingers in the wrong places and losing an eye and wearing life jackets on the log barges and so on. Norm listened patiently as I shared how people seemed to be rewarded for unsafe behavior. I began to notice he was listening intently. He was focused on every word I spoke.

After I told him my fears, he walked through every single one of them and told me why it was best to follow the rules and that I would never get fired if I worked safely. He also said, "If you come across a situation where you don't know what to do, then you need to stop. You will never get in trouble for stopping. I would rather you stop then go and get hurt."

That day I realized how much Norman cared about his company. I realized how much he cared about his people. Although I never knew what he said in the office when he left me out in the yard that July day, I have been able to piece together certain details from people who were there.

Norm went in there and asked the guys why it took me to step up and say something. No one was in trouble, but he wanted every single guy to understand how they would have done the same thing if they had been listening to all this negative energy. He saved my life that day. No wonder no one killed me. He wouldn't let them, and he made them realize they were partly to blame.

Then he got people to speak up, which I hadn't been able to do. So, in a sense, they got their beefs out in the open through my naïveté. Right end result, wrong path to get there.

What if I hadn't been a stupid kid that day and spoke up the way I did? Norman's talk with me provided some enlightenment. He made me more aware of "how to do the job right." Maybe that talk kept other people on the worksite from making the wrong decisions. Either way, right end result, wrong path.

Looking back, the issue was that we were rewarded far too often for taking chances. As I mentioned previously, when leaders continue to give positive reinforcement for the wrong behavior, it will cause individuals to keep making similar choices. Instead of reinforcing the wrong behavior, leadership needs to set the tone and lead by positive example.

People often ask, "Is a leader who says one thing and does the opposite leading by example?" The answer most groups give when I ask this question is, "That's *not* leading by example," but it is. It is leading by the wrong example. Workers see leadership doing the opposite of what they are told, so how can the leader possibly influence the group effectively?

Instead of leadership giving a negative consequence to the worker who makes the right choice, we need to see positive reinforcement of the safe choice. This will influence people to continue making the safe behavioral choices, and this message gets mixed up far too often.

Chapter Seven
The Four Cornerstones

Optimization is a word that gets thrown around a lot. Say it out loud, slowly. It sounds complicated and almost sexy. Optimization is *key* to any business survival, and whether it's a logging company or a drilling company or an energy production company, if the business can't optimize, then it will suffer and ultimately disappear.

When looking back on my career in forestry, I recall several occasions when I vividly remember optimization as I understood it then. When I worked in the log yard my first summer, I just didn't do one task, I did many, and some of them all at once. I took the used paint cans to the garbage fire, coiled the unused wire, stamped the ends of the scaled logs with a log mark, recorded and retrieved tag numbers from the log bundles, wrapped the tags into a tight file, and then recorded the data in the log bundle dump log.

These tasks has been performed previously by two people, but when the logging margins got tight, that meant people needed to optimize and multitask so efficiency and productivity went up.

It was no different in oil and gas operations in western Canada. It was a work expectation that we as managers optimize our equipment or people. If we had a chemical truck that was doing a job for a client next to another client's lease, we loaded more chemicals into the truck than the one client needed. When done with the first job, we would go to the second, and charge the truck out as if it had left town and drove all the way out. This common practice is also referred to as "double dipping," and as managers in the oil and gas service industry we were expected to optimize the maximum use of equipment and people. Optimization meant more money, period.

So what is it that we optimize in business? Or, for a better way to look at it, "What are we supposed to manage in business and then optimize?"

I had many conversations with managers in my career where we shared ideas about what managers should manage. I never really thought that business could be broken down effectively in a model or example until I was exposed to one by a fellow leadership facilitator and colleague of mine, Mr. Glenn Morasch, in the spring of 2008.

Glenn shared what he called "the four cornerstones of the business model" in a session I was co-facilitating with him in Calgary for the one of the world's largest energy companies. He worked the model in front of Canadian business managers for this energy client and drew four boxes on a flip chart and asked a series of questions to get the answers from the group.

What he worked through were the four key aspects of any business. These are money, production, time, and health safety and environment (HSE). He got the people in the room to uncover each aspect for themselves by putting it into "their" business routine, thereby making it real. The end result was the first three were identified quite easily, while the last, HSE, required some probing in the group to get them to realize how important HSE aspects really are to the success and ultimate survival of any business. It was a revelation for me and the group just how often they had put money ahead of HSE, and so often had succeeded.

This model got me thinking. If we don't manage money, production, time, and HSE properly, there isn't any business or future business. As this group of leaders were voicing their approval that indeed we required all four of those cornerstones to be successful in business, Glenn hit them with a cannon blast.

He stopped them in their tracks when he pointed to the four boxes and asked the question, "Which one of these boxes have we elevated the importance of in our careers?" The participants almost all stopped breathing simultaneously. Dead silence followed. People just stared at the four boxes and kept perfectly quiet. The most senior leader in the room, a vice president, finally spoke after ten to fifteen seconds of silence and said, "I can tell you I have placed the money box ahead of all the others on many occasions in my career."

Then this VP went on further, "I was sitting here working through all four of the boxes and realized that I have prioritized three of the four boxes differently on many different occasions, and the ugly end result is that HSE finished last far too often."

People in the room began to slowly nod their approval to this explanation. I was at the back of the room, watching and listening. I remembered my first job at Norman's log yard and it all made sense. We were placing a priority on HSE, but we needed it to be a value. Priorities change, values seldom do. No wonder we dodged so many bullets and struggled with safety results so much. Safety was a priority that we rearranged when it conflicted with money, production, and time.

They needed to be in balance, and when people's safety was at risk, the HSE box of the four cornerstones needed to trump the other three. I reviewed an entire career of decisions I had made both in the energy services sector and the forest industry and realized I had not given HSE the value it deserved. It was a terrible revelation to discover that I had not made safety a value and I had failed to balance the four cornerstones.

What if I had been exposed to the four cornerstones model years earlier? My god, the changes I could have made in my life. Not just for my safety, but the safety of others.

Knowing the cornerstones was one of those "penny drops" that needed to happen for me to write this book. I recognized that I had prioritized many things in my career, but the four cornerstones model put clarity to an "unknown" knowledge I needed it long ago. If I had known the "value based" culture and did everything I could to get there, maybe things would have been different.

Chapter Eight
No Longer Just a
Summer Student

As mentioned back a bit, I worked three more summers at the log yard. I graduated high school in 1989 and went away to college in the Vancouver area and got a couple of math classes and geography classes I needed for my end goal, which was to be a pilot. It took a year of these courses for me to have the required curriculum to get my commercial pilot's license.

Most of my life I either wanted to be a pilot or the passenger of an airplane. I am not kidding with the last statement. My mom tells the funny tale of how when I was three or four years old, people would ask me what I wanted to do when I grew up, and I always said, "Be a passenger in an airplane."

That is ironic, because as I travel the world as leadership consultant at least two days a week to different locations across North America. I usually fly on a Monday and a Friday as a passenger in an airplane. Wow.

Working in that log yard got me into college. Not the grades part, but it gave me the money to pay for the schooling. I actually spent five summers working in that log yard. Norman had taken a shine to me, and although I had a lot of negative characteristics, he kept letting me come back.

As each summer would go by he would let me operate the heavier equipment and I learned lots of new tasks. Eventually I went back in what I thought was going to be my final summer and he began to give me a lot of responsibility. I was supervising guys and helping with work schedules. It was great. I figured this was going to be my last summer because I was finishing flight training and it would be time to start my new career.

In that last summer I had great talks with Norman. When I started to work for him five years back I was a fifteen-year-old kid. I had grown up a bit (not enough) and he told me as I left that summer that if I needed to come back he would make a position for me. What a great way to send me off. It was a great job.

Norman and Linda's company used float planes a lot. They had logging camps at different places along the coast of British Columbia, and Norman had said if I ever wanted to come back and fly for him that he would lease a plane and I could get my hours with him. Business man to the end. He knew if I did this it would mean he could use my license to fly guys around, and I would lower his business costs significantly and he could use me for other jobs when not flying. Smart man.

I learned so much about working with different equipment in the log yard, but it wasn't the only place I worked for Norman. He had helicopter logging operations and conventional high lead or tower operations as well. Each of these operations utilized different equipment. Logging trucks, log loaders, rubber tired front end loaders, tractors, excavators, and of course boats and barges of all sizes and types.

I frequently found myself out on log tows in the middle of the coast. I would be miles from nowhere on a slow log tow, where you tow a huge amount of logs from one spot to another using the marine channels. Usually these log tows would take three or four days because the camps the logs came out of were up to one hundred miles from Prince Rupert. There were no roads running along the coast of BC. Imagine the vast coastline with no towns or cities for miles. This is where you got see nature at its finest.

I saw killer whales, sea otters, seals, bald eagles, all sorts of fish, bears, and wolves. I got to spend each summer in this environment. It was heaven. Every so often Norman would let me go and spend a few days in the logging camp. I would go in and cover for somebody who needed days off. What a sight that was.

Logging spars called towers and grapple yarders and helicopters flew all over these logging blocks. You haven't seen anything until you've seen a big logging show underway. Men and machines, moving logs off of steep mountainsides. Some logging blocks were completed by using a logging tower. Other blocks would use helicopters. The helicopter logging was a sight to behold.

These huge helicopters would fly in with a 150-foot long cable underneath it and gently drop that hook onto a mountainside with inches of an awaiting hooker that would hook a turn of logs up to the helicopter. Then the guy who just hooked the logs to this 150-foot cable that was hanging off a helicopter would run like hell up a hillside out of harm's way.

That helicopter would lift the logs down to a water drop and let them off into the water, where another operator running around in a boat would race to the logs to retrieve the chokers before the chopper returned in about sixty seconds with another turn of logs. They would do this dance all day. Not stopping except for when the helicopter needed to refuel (which was about every hour) or go through the midday shut down for maintenance.

The most amazing thing I have seen in my whole life around work was the precision that went into pulling helicopter logging off all day, every day. This amazing feat was almost matched by the tower logging crews that pulled logs off mountain slopes every day the same as the helicopters. Either way, this stuff was amazing.

I would spend a few days here and there in these camps and then have to go back to reality. I'll never forget the day I was getting off the float plane at one of the camps down near an area called Union Pass. I was getting off the plane, and as I got onto the camp dock I looked up and saw this tough, giant of a man standing there holding his eye. I could tell that he was covering up a pretty good cut because there was blood (a lot of blood) all over his collar and work shirt. I knew this guy, his name was Wendell. He used to work at the log sort yard here and there bucking the wood. That is when you take a chainsaw and cut the logs to paint lines that a scaler puts on them. He was a funny, crazy man.

Wendell's regular job was that of a faller. A faller was the one of the guys who ran around the mountainside with a chainsaw, cutting down the trees. This job is very dangerous. There may be those who think this is simple. It is not. Imagine trying to cut down a tree on mountainside, which is sometimes very steep. This tree could be as high as one hundred feet. This tree generally grows straight up, but there is always a slight tilt to the tree, and when these trees are to be felled they all need to be felled the same way, so that they are all in neat rows.

That makes it easier to grab the logs off the hillside with the helicopter or the grapple yarder.

It is no easy task. So I get off the plane and there is Wendell. As I ask him what's happened, thinking it's just a cut, he pulls his hand away from his eye along with the towel that was all red, and I saw a terrible sight. Wendell revealed a stick jabbed into his eye socket. I don't mean a little stick, either. This piece of wood was about one inch around and was probably three to four inches embedded in his eye socket.

I was not expecting that. He was standing there as if nothing was wrong and hardly showing any ill effects, and he had a stick lodged into his eye socket. He looked okay, yet I felt as if I were going to pass out. I asked him again what happened, and he said, "Nothing."

I pushed him a little and he told me he slipped while walking on a log as he was cutting the branches off and as he did he fell face first onto the stick that was now stuck in his eye socket. The interesting part here is that it obviously hurt and his eyeball was looking a little different than normal. His eyeball was intact, but it wasn't circular anymore. It was now more egg-like. It was being pushed into a slightly different shape than the usual eye we see.

His eye socket was a mess, however. It was torn open, and when I look back it is kind of humorous, but imagine this man who could not move his eyeball so he had to turn to look by moving his whole body. It was much like the guy or gal who strains their neck, so they turn their whole body to look at you. That's not the funny part. Imagine he has to turn to see things and then he has about six inches of a stick probing straight out from his eye socket.

Funny, but gross. This seemed to happen way too much. It seemed every time I was asked to go fill in at the logging camp it was because of someone getting injured. I wasn't always the first guy who got called to fill in when someone was injured. Norman used to keep track of who went in to cover for the injured, and he kept it pretty fair, but I am not kidding that it seemed like every week someone was getting flown in to work for some guy who got hurt.

This is where I identified my first trend.

Chapter Nine
Work Site Trends

As I flew into this camp every so often during my summers, I begin to see that there was a trend in the number and timing of the injuries. These guys that worked in the camps worked a twenty-one-day in and a seven-day out shift. So if I had to ask you when the injuries occurred (which days out of the twenty-one-day shift), what would you say?

My initial thoughts before recognizing this trend was that the guys must get hurt in the middle of the shift because that's when they become complacent in their tasks. I was wrong. I was basing my theory on my limited experience in the workforce. Parents have been banging their heads off walls since the beginning of time as young adults like me who think they have all the answers base our answers on a narrow-minded thought process. The reality is that the workers are usually injured at the beginning of the shift (on days one, two, or three), and then the injuries seem to go away until the last three or four days before crew change.

My theory of complacency was wrong. I thought that workers would be most aware after coming back because they were refreshed and ready to go and weren't distracted by events at camp, in a sense because they were happy. The reality was most guys would go out on days off and catch up one of a few things. Either family time, or things that resemble how to make a family.

Chasing the ladies was a common practice of the younger guys in their mid twenties or so. Guys who had been married suddenly found themselves not married, partly because they were out of town in these camps frequently and also because these men developed bad habits with money, and that is a stress that isn't easily managed.

Drinking was rampant outside of the camps. Most camps were dry, meaning that alcohol and drugs were not allowed, but I am not so naive to say that drugs weren't being used in the camps.

So as I came to a slowly educated understanding through my experiences surrounding these injury patterns, I thought I should tell Norman. Here was an opportunity to show my intelligence. So when the opportunity presented itself, I went to him and asked this question. "Hey, Norman, when do you think your people are getting hurt on their shifts?" I was ready to share my knowledge and inform Norman of a trend I was positive he didn't understand.

He looked at me with a smile and said, "First couple of days and last couple of days."

Okay, Norman was smarter than I thought. I never thought he was unintelligent. I just didn't think he really bothered to understand the trend in relation to work shifts. I couldn't have been more wrong. I sat there for about fifteen minutes (on his dime) while he explained to me that guys' heads are still in town when they get to camp. For a few of the guys it takes them a couple of days to get certain drugs out of their system. For some it isn't drugs, but it is wondering what the girlfriend may be up to while they are in camp, and for others still it is missing their children or wife or perhaps wondering about a loved one who may be sick or dying.

These distractions pull the workers' attention from the work. People don't purposely put themselves in harm's way, but they don't recognize that they are in harm's way until ... BANG, they get hurt. Please remember also that these guys are in a camp that is remote. Norman's camps were usually seventy-five miles from Prince Rupert. The only way in or out was by float plane or boat. That also contributed to the uneasiness, because if something went wrong in camp, it is hard to get to town to help or fix a family emergency. And this was way before cell phones. The only communication with loved ones was through a two-way radio system and everyone could hear the conversation on the entire coast in other camps or villages or boats.

The other side to Norman's explanation was that near the end of a twenty-one day shift guys are tired and their thoughts are returning to home. For some it was anticipation of seeing the wife and kids again. For others it was the thought of going home and maybe having to go to the bank and get finances figured out (for good or bad) and for others it was what trouble they could get themselves into. Either way, Norman had this figured out bang on.

I must have looked funny because he continued to smile and asked why I was asking.

I explained that I had noticed the trend of guys getting hurt early and late in the shift and that my original theory was way off. Norman smiled again (he wasn't always smiling), and he explained why he needed to know when the injuries occurred. He explained how he had to pay a percentage of every payroll dollar to the Worker's Compensation Board to insure the workers should they have an injury.

He went on to further explain that he tries to do the tasks that are less risky earlier in the shift. This man didn't go to a safety training school to get educated. He *was* a safety training school. His company was similar to so many and I am sure now when I reflect on this that almost every other company owner had the same knowledge within their company. They didn't pay to go to school and learn about safety, they were living and breathing safety all day every day.

In fact, Norman's business was heavily safety based. It wasn't something he sold as goods, and maybe that was part of the problem. To properly manage his business he would have to balance the four cornerstones of business, but if "optimizing" meant people were making the wrong behavior choices, it could mean the four cornerstones of business would be in conflict with each other.

Let's say that I had three or four tasks to do in order to finish the day. These tasks all would normally take thirty minutes each. To perform all three or four at once meant I may have to cut a corner or two (or more), so I begin to rationalize this internally. My statement already has indicated that I am probably going to unbalance the four boxes.

In order to maintain production, and spend less time (which means more profit), I begin to cut corners, like ignoring a procedure that is designed to keep me safe, or worse, I work around an engineered guard so I can finish faster. I have placed priority on three of the four boxes in the cornerstones model at the sacrifice of the HSE box.

To make matters worse, when I did this in Norman's company, he would support the choices "if no one got hurt" with an atta boy. When that happens a clear signal has been sent. Do it as long as you don't get caught. There will be positive rewards, and as we know, if the wrong behavior is supported, the chances of doing it again will most definitely increase.

Norman may have understood the cost of safety to his bottom line, but he also understood optimization and its effect on the four cornerstones. In fact, who do you think took more chances than anyone else in the company with their personal behavior?

Norman always told us, "Don't do what I do," but if he was doing it, then it became our expectation of ourselves. Although he talked a great game, he also took many risks and threw boxes of the cornerstones out of balance far too often.

He was leading by example. What kind of example was Norman setting? What behaviors would we chose based on his leadership?

Chapter Ten
The Four Cornerstones and Risk

Money, production, time and health, safety, and the environment. Norman was in the logging business, but as part of properly managing his company, it meant he was also in the safety business. Safety wasn't a revenue stream. He did not sell safety. Norman sold logs or logging services, but his ability to sell logs or services depended on his company being able to prove its value with safety as a key business driver.

Every time Norm's company had an incident, his Worker's Compensation Premiums went up, so if the company was not effectively managing the behaviors of its workforce, it meant that costs would go up substantially. The other negative for not managing safety effectively is that logging companies perform very dangerous work and unfortunately there are fatalities.

Fatalities don't just happen. They happen for many reasons, but a key one is that safe work actions are not used. An individual chooses an unsafe behavior, and many times he or she gets away with it. If there are no negative consequences, the worker continues the at risk behavior and escalates it. After hundreds and maybe even thousands of these actions, the safety filters line up to allow an unacceptable amount of risk exposure through to the individual.

The result of this misalignment is often a disaster, and ultimately an incident or fatality. Let's be honest, every single one of us has performed tens of thousands of unsafe acts in our lifetimes. Whether at work or at play, the fact is we do it. Proof of this is that almost all of us drive, and driving is dangerous. Just look all the features built into an automobile that are designed to lessen the impact of not *"if"* but *"when"* we will be in a car accident.

Airbags, headlights, antilock brakes, traction control, seatbelts, windshields, tires, crumple zones ... the list goes on and on. Similar features are built into smart businesses. These filters act to lessen the severity of the consequences through reducing the probability of the act occurring, which is why there are so many systems in place to reduce the probability.

I always get a rush when facilitating this discussion with energy managers in my consultancy role. What I have just described is commonly referred to as the risk equation, where the following is rolled out to a group.

RISK = CONSEQUENCE x LIKELIHOOD

Let's write the explanation like this Risk (loaded gun) = Consequence (death) x Likelihood (one bullet for six chambers). There you have it, taken from the horrible example of Russian roulette. The risk is the loaded gun, the consequences are death if the gun is pointed at one's head playing Russian roulette. The reason people will play (if they are crazy), is because there are six chambers on a thirty-eight caliber pistol and only one bullet. The likelihood of the consequence occurring are one in six. Statistically, a 83.33 percent chance if you are the first to play that you will pull the trigger on a blank chamber.

Ironically, the chances of the chamber being chosen with the bullet in it go up each time an empty chamber is triggered. The likelihood increases of the bullet being fired after each person pulls the trigger on an empty chamber. The likelihood of the consequence occurring is now going up until ultimately the bullet is fired.

Let's stick with the vehicle example and all the safety filters installed in every vehicle. What if we just had antilock brakes, and not airbags? Antilock brakes are great, but the braking system is a single safety filter that is attempting to manipulate the likelihood side of the equation to our favor.

Would you rather drive in a vehicle on a busy highway or interstate when people were travelling at seventy-five miles an hour with only antilock brakes as your means of protection? Of course not. Our modern vehicles have many filters in place to minimize the likelihood of the incident. Some of the safety filters, such as the airbag, are even designed to minimize the consequences resulting from the formula and its statistical relevance.

Safety filters in a logging company begin with the behaviors of people utilizing the safety management system. These are the policies or procedures. There is the engineer guarding to prevent the machine and human interface, a preventative maintenance system of checks and balances, and then of course the final filter of personal protective equipment.

What I learned right there standing on a mountainside talking to Norman, was that although he was in the logging business, he was also in the safety business. Not to sell safety as a revenue stream, but to have a level of safety to ensure the revenue stream was protected. As I worked my way through several types of businesses during my career, I often thought about the lessons I learned from Norman. Many of the training classes and courses I took showed me that Norman knew the value of safety better than any book.

Norman educated me that summer day. I gained a knowledge of him that I didn't have before, I learned about safety in business that I didn't know before, and I began to understand at age twenty that maybe I should start listening more to people who have years of experience because they seemed to have it figured out and I didn't.

As he explained to me, everyone in the operation managed risk. We all had to actively and visibly manage that risk, not only for ourselves, but for others, or there was a dam good chance that someone would get hurt.

Being risk aware was not always easy, however. In logging companies, or energy companies, or whatever company, the business must make money through time management and production goals to stay afloat. In many cases, the priority (notice I didn't say value) of production that ensures profit indicates that the HSE component of the four cornerstones is eroded.

An example is a routine task. We manage the risk associated with that routine task all day, every day. We begin to wrongly associate that spending too much time in the pre-planning or risk recognition stage indicates that we are losing time from actually getting the job done, which ultimately costs our business money. If we aren't making money, we aren't productive. If we aren't productive, we are going to be out of business, fast.

Almost every worker feels the stress of production. Whether real or

41

perceived, we feel it. Perception becomes reality, and when push comes to shove, we start looking for the ability to increase or maximize money. The first cornerstone we typically look to chip away at is HSE.

We then begin to sacrifice the collective safety of the workforce by taking a little less time (optimizing) in safety sensitive situations. We lower our risk tolerance, and we continue to do this by minimizing the safety filter's effectiveness until we experience some type of loss.

After we have lowered our risk tolerance and sacrificed safety, we stand around after an incident and ask silly questions like, "How did this happen?"

Chapter Eleven
What are You Laughing At? Get That Boat

The personal revelation on managing risk as it related to business and behaviors from the last chapter was one I look back on fondly. I recall it vividly as I work with people around North America talking about motivation and workplace leadership. The day I asked Norman about whether he understood his company trends and where we were at risk, he could have looked at me and said something along the lines of, "I don't pay you to talk with me about safety," and went on his way. He was always busy. He had this monster company that had operations in different areas. He was always flying or driving somewhere, yet he gave me the time to talk with him about safety. He was trying to create the "want-to" in me to work safely.

I wondered why back then, but I don't wonder anymore. I realized years later that when Norman gave me the fifteen minutes to talk with him about safety, that he was activating a behavior in me. I could have shared my original theory about when guys are at their best in a twenty-one day shift, and even if I was wrong, Norman would have then talked to me about his experiences and through that he would have educated me. Through that education he would have given me a greater understanding of his company's workplace safety and I would have shared that with other people onsite, and everyone would be safer.

What was really interesting was Norman wasn't always this warm and fuzzy guy. That man could peel paint with foul language. He didn't just lose his temper, he lost his mind when he lost his temper. He only ever got mad when people wouldn't or couldn't do what was supposed to be done, but when he went off ... oh my god.

One day I watched him get into an argument with one of his sons, Jason. Imagine how this goes. You can already piece together from the man I described that he would be harder on his sons than anyone else. One day Norman and Jason weren't agreeing on something out on the log boom, and they started arguing.

They were standing on these log bundles floating on the water, and Norman was yelling at Jason. He was yelling so much that as they argued, the boat that they were using to put the log bundles away floated away on them. I was standing back about thirty feet on another log bundle that was already lashed to a boom stick and then to shore. To me, this was hilarious. They were yelling about the right way to do a task and their only mode of transport was drifting away from them.

Norman's skin was a red color that couldn't have been healthy, and a vein was showing on his forehead. Jason was at the point of disgust where he was ignoring his dad altogether. Norman blurted out this gem of a line to Jason in his anger, "Listen, you son of a f#%$*ng whore, you better start listening to me! I don't care what you think, my way is the right way."   Now I don't know how Jason kept his thoughts together enough to come up with this response, but it was brilliant and dangerous all at the same time. Jason said, "When I tell mom you called her a f#%$*ng whore, she is going to kick your ass." Argument over.

Jason had successfully fired a shot into Norman's wheelhouse and Norman realized it. They just stopped talking. The two of them stood there in a silent faceoff. Norman took definite pride in being a man's man, but no matter how much of a hard ass he could be, he didn't want to tangle with Linda. There was no way he could win that confrontation.

So here was a father and his son who hadn't solved a thing yelling at each other, and they started to look around to go back to work. Once they realized that they had floated away from their boat, they almost simultaneously looked at each other and started laughing. This could have gone from tense to tenser in seconds, but it didn't. Norman and Jason started laughing uncontrollably. They were laughing pretty hard, and so I started laughing because the tension was leaving and this was good in my mind.

They were laughing and I was wondering how this was going work out, when Norman looked up while still laughing and said, "Dwayne, go get that boat for us." They started laughing even harder because I would have to swim to it, just as they would have. I was probably a little closer to it than them, but they let the boat drift away. Why should I have to go get it? Norman was pulling rank.

Why should the owner, the president of this logging company, have to be accountable for his mistakes, right? They were laughing furiously now. They were bent over in hysterics when Jason yelped out, "What is taking you so long?" I am fearful they may pass out because they are laughing so hard.

So while they laugh away I figured I better get the boat, because chances are slim that Norman or his son will jump in. I dove in and swam to it. I thought they couldn't possibly laugh any harder, but when I got to the boat they were in stitches. They were both sitting down on the bundle because they were laughing so hard. Jason was actually crying. Through tears he declared to me, "Seriously, Dwayne, I didn't mean for you to jump in! I was going to get it!"

I got the boat to them and we all calmed down and got back to normal. I asked to go to camp to change my clothes because they were all wet. Norm turned to me and said with a smile, "Not a chance, that is ten minutes away." Jason and Norman start laughing again, and they walked away from me, and I realized he was serious. See, I told you he was a hard ass.

So there it is. Norman wasn't perfect. The one thing I really need to convey about Norman is that when it came to managing his company, he *almost* always tried to do it safely. In fact, Norman told me before I went off to flight training that I would have to ensure that I always did the task right, because if I didn't take the time to do it right on the ground, then I wouldn't get the time to get it right up in the air. Norman's heart was huge, and I witnessed people take advantage of him several times.

Chapter Twelve
Who is This Tough Guy?

Norman's tough exterior was a front for the big softie that was behind the tough exterior. Please don't go thinking that he was a fraud, far from it. He used to really lose it, and there were some people who were fearful of his blasts. The truth of the matter was he was only ever mad or frustrated when people failed to make the right decisions, which in his mind broke down into two categories.

One, work safely.

Two, work safely until you needed to work at risk in order to get the job done.

Hopefully you can see the dilemma for workers in this situation. Norman wanted a good safety record, because that meant a good business foundation, but he also wanted optimization, which meant that he often supported unsafe behavioral choices.

I remember clearly a day when he and I were working together moving equipment onto one of the company barges. Norman's company was diverse, and moving his own equipment saved thousands of dollars.

What was really interesting was he always seemed the most upset when someone hurt themselves. He would always ask first, "Is everyone okay?" From there he would start to work the issue backwards, and if the end result was somebody was hurt because they chose to cut a corner and were injured ... oh boy.

In truth, anyone who worked for Norman longer than six months fell in love with him. He was hard on people, but he was only really holding them accountable. I didn't always see it this way. I thought on many occasions that people never knew the care he had for his workers.

Let me share an example. There was an employee of Norman's who was always having trouble with drugs. This guy used to abuse anything from marijuana to cocaine to heroine to alcohol. Sometimes this guy would even mix some of those substances together and go to work. He always got caught. It isn't easy to prove when someone is taking those drugs. To just blurt out that you think someone is on them could get you in a lot of trouble.

This employee would get caught by Norman, and he would have to fire this guy. This happened at least twice while I worked for Norm. He would never tell anyone why the guy was gone. He never violated anyone's privacy. He was always showing respect for this man, no matter the issue. Here is something I found out later.

One payday I went over to Norman and Linda's house to pick up my paycheck, and there was this former employee who had been fired for substance abuse walking up to the front door. I hadn't see him in a bit and asked where he had been. Now I was used to seeing this guy look like crap. When he was using he was a mess. He looked terrible, smelled bad, and just looked like he could die any second. Yet here he was standing on the front walk looking great.

Before either of us could knock on the door it opened up and Norman invited us in. He looked very happy to see this other guy. Norman commented on how good he looked and even brought me into the conversation, asking if I noticed, too. Of course I did. This guy smiled and thanked us, and then the unexpected happened. This former employee became a new employee. Norman looked at him and said, "You must be here for your job back. Done."

I never knew a deal was made. How would I? Norman never talked to anyone else about conversations he had with people. This guy was smiling, and Norman put his arm around him and said, "I couldn't be prouder of you." This guy then broke down crying and thanked Norman. I was standing there feeling a little uncomfortable because I was unsure if I should be there. Norman looked up at me with a tear in his eye and just hugged this man. The guy just sobbed, saying, "Thank you" over and over again.

Norman told him, "You don't need to thank me. You kicked the drugs, not me." Then this is really interesting part that I remember fondly forever. This man reached into his pocket and pulled out a wad of money. He handed it Norman and said, "It is all there, every penny I borrowed from you to go to rehab." Holy shit. Norman had paid for this guy to go to rehab, even after he fired him. Not only had he paid for the rehab, Norman had lent this man money to pay his bills while he was in rehab. I never knew all the details, because Norman never told anyone about his dealings with people, but Norman showed me what true caring looked like that day, and it was pure coincidence that I saw it.

Just when I thought that Norman's caring couldn't go any further, Norman took the money from this guy and looked him straight in the eye and said, "Where did you get all this from? You haven't worked in a while." The man explained that it meant so much to him to get the money back to Norman for taking a chance on him that he took some stuff to the pawn shop to get Norman the money.

Norman pulled him back in and gave him a bear hug. He then looked at this guy again and said, "How much do you need to get by for the next month?" You can already picture where this is going. Norman peeled back about half that money and gave it back to him. Norman told this man to take that money back and get food for the refrigerator, buy some new work clothes, and be at work Monday morning ready to go.

The guy thanked Norman again, and as I sat there staring at this exchange, I was overwhelmed. I was standing there alone with Norman on his front steps. I didn't know what to say. I was just there to pick up a paycheck, and I witnessed the kindest act of my young life.

Norman looked at me as the truck pulled out of the driveway and said with a stern look, "Not a word to anyone, Dwayne, do you understand? Not a word to anyone."

I knew the reasons why, or so I thought. I said, "I know you don't want anyone to know your soft side."

Norman looked at with me with a little bit of concern and said, "Soft side, Dwayne, I don't care about that. I don't want anyone to know what you saw here just now because it would be disrespectful of you to talk about that man and his troubles." I was already amazed by the kindness I saw minutes before, and now I am amazed at my stupidity.

Norman must have seen the embarrassment on my face. He reached up and put his arm around me and said with a smile, "You are too young to know how this plays out. Don't feel bad. Learn from this. You never talk about someone else." As my embarrassment started to go away, we talked for a few moments, and then Norman asked why I dropped by. I told him I was there to pick up my paycheck. He looked at me and said, "I just gave back that guy all that money, so I will have to pay you later."

The look on my face must have been something. I looked at Norman and he looked very serious, so I got ready to turn around and go. Then he let out a huge barrel laugh and handed me my check. What a guy, funny to the end. As I laughed with him for a few moments, we exchanged pleasantries and I began to walk away. I got a few steps down the front walk, and Norman barked, "Dwayne, not a word to anyone!" I turned to look at him and acknowledge his final request.

It has been years since Norman and I talked. I'm only sharing what I saw on his front steps to prove the caring man he was. I never mentioned our friend's name and never will. I learned more about leadership and respect that day on his front steps than I could my entire life. I never shared that story until now.

Chapter Thirteen
Flight School and Reality

Later in the summer of 1990 I went to flight training school near Vancouver. What an experience. It cost a small fortune to get my commercial pilot's license if you added room and board into the equation. Who am I kidding; it was a large fortune.

I wasn't simply going to flight school to get my private license. I could get that license for about five thousand dollars back then. I wanted my commercial license, which meant I needed many more flight hours. Then I would need a commercial license that had the night rating attached to it, a float endorsement, a multi-engine endorsement, and eventually a turbine rating and then an instrument flight rating, and so on and so on.

This little bit of education was going to cost me about fifteen thousand dollars. Okay, I am kidding, it was going to cost me fifteen thousand bucks, but it was going to cost my parents a few more dollars than that, about thirty thousand more dollars than what I had. That's what parents were for, right? I had saved the money from the four months working for Norman. But I had to go my mom and dad for the amount I needed. They had put money away for my education my entire life, but they didn't have thirty thousand dollars.

The idea was for me to go to flight school and get a part-time job down there and help get the end goal accomplished. I figured if I went and got a part-time job, I might make it. If I didn't manage to get all my training accomplished in one year, I could go back and work logging for another summer. Norman had offered me a job next year if I needed it. I wanted to keep that door open.

So I started flight training and it went really well. I got my private pilot's license and started to work on building up my flight time. I took ground school and started my other endorsements. I got the commercial license done pretty quickly and was ready to take on the world and sit back and make $125,000 per year as a chief pilot, but there was a snag ... reality.

I started to send out resumes before I even finished the training, and no one called me in for an interview. I even phoned a few companies to ask if they got my resume and they put me on hold. They'd go away for a few minutes and come back to me and say, "Yeah, we got it."

"What did you think of my resume?" I'd ask.

The answer that usually came back was, "Did we phone you?"

Wow ... that was tough. It is also reality. Welcome to the real world. I was raised in a generation where parents started concerning themselves with the "self-esteem" of the generation. This has benefits, but we are now seeing a generation that can't handle real feedback. One of the things that my experiences showed was that workers only tended to hear from management when things went wrong. So if you didn't hear from the management it meant, "Keep up the good work."

The interesting thing about feedback is we need it to thrive. Feedback is commonly on any list that is centered around the traits of a great leader. The organization I work with that travels around the world doing leadership training for the major oil and gas companies has made lists of the traits of a great leader based on feedback from around the continent. The list, no matter where it is drawn from, no matter in what language, almost always looks the same.

I bring up the power of feedback because Norman shared with me his concern a few times when I was growing up how I was too eager to put myself at risk to complete a task. He took me aside on more than one occasion to remind me on how to do a job safely. He was trying to correct my behavior. Instead of yelling and screaming at me, which he did do once in a while, he would coach me. I always took more away from the coaching than the yelling.

So when the human resources departments I talked to at the airlines told me that maybe I needed to start applying at smaller regional carriers and not the large international air carriers, I was upset. However, I also recognized that these people were giving me feedback that I could chose to listen to or ignore. If I listened to the feedback, chances are I could use it for career development. Some of those people I talked to on the phone actually told me who was hiring and who specifically to call.

I got great career leads from listening to people and behaving accordingly. I kept listening to people's advice and called the smaller carriers, but I was still finding it difficult to land a job. This trend went on and on for a few weeks. As each day went on, I realized that I was running out of money. So where is the first place a twenty-year-old goes when he can't find a job? You guessed it ... I called mom and dad. I was sure they wanted to help out.

I called Dad and talked about other things first, the weather and all that crap. Dad must have sensed something was up. He asked me, "What's up?" I finally told him that I was almost out of money and could I borrow a few thousand dollars until my career takes off? The phone went quiet. So quiet, in fact, that I had to ask Dad if he was still there. He was. He came back with an answer that wasn't quite what I was expecting.

Dad explained very slowly that he could do that, but it would not really be fair to them. Fair to them? What was this about? So I asked what he meant, and my father said that he and my mom had worked hard over the last few years, and I wasn't really trying to get my career going by giving up. If I needed money, the best option was to either find work in Vancouver flying or I could get a non-flying job down there until I did find a flying job. The last and least popular option for me was that I could go home to Prince Rupert and maybe get a job working with Norman's company for another summer and bank that money and then go and search for that flying job with money in the bank.

Remember before when I said my parents had raised me to be logical and think things through? What a bunch of crap. Truth be told, I had a feeling that my parents had an idea this was happening to me. They were just a little too prepared with the perfect answers to my call. Logical thinking. Mom and dad knew I was calling and were prepared. They outflanked me.

So I moved back to Prince Rupert, and before moving back I called Norman. He was happy to have me back. He even answered my asking for the job with, "I told you if you needed to work for me to just show up," another life lesson that I was thankful for right then and there.

I was back with friends from high school and working the summer and saving tidy sums of money away for my move back to Vancouver in a few months. I started realizing that there would be a lot of money in logging if I made a career out of it. I was making about nineteen dollars per hour in that summer of 1991. I got to chatting with Norman one day about when I was thinking of moving back, and I mentioned that I may stay on till Christmas to save up even more money. He said no problem if that's what I wanted.

One must remember that I was typically exposed to summer operations when it came to logging. I had worked for five summers and this was the sixth. I had helped out during a couple of Christmas holidays for a couple of weeks when Norman had work to do in the warehouse. That typically consisted of cutting wire to be used for chokers (chokers were twenty-foot-long wires that had a bell and knob on the end that were used behind cats or skidders), or sometimes I would cut helicopter logging chokers which were about twenty feet long also, but they had to have the eye spliced in them. I was never really exposed to the elements.

I hope you remember earlier when I said Prince Rupert is famous for two things. One is salmon fishing, the other is rain. The rain in the late spring and summer is bearable, it doesn't rain as hard as the winter and fall. Also, the temperature is just above freezing for nearly six months, and when it does fall below zero it snows a terrible amount in a short period of time and it causes no good whatsoever.

The reason I share this little tidbit is because the fall of 1991 was the first time I had worked in the logging industry full time. What a mess. It started raining mid-September that year and did not stop until after winter way out into March. Sure there were a few days where it was just cloudy, even a few days when the sun broke through the clouds, but it poured.

I began to work primarily on water operations once I went full time. Norman had a logging operation along the Skeena river at a place called Windsor Creek. It was about a thirty-five minute drive from Prince Rupert, and then we had to cross the river in boats to the other side.

I ended up being pretty good at booming. As mentioned earlier, that is when bundles of logs are put into a log rack. One could typically get twenty big logs into this rack. When I say "big," I mean about two feet in diameter or larger and about forty-five feet long. All these logs in the rack would be strapped together with wire cables so it was tight and then pushed into the water. It more or less looked like a perfectly floating log raft once it was floating.

These log bundles were then stowed in rows and held together by boom sticks. These boom sticks were usually sixty feet long and three feet wide (big, long, and sturdy), and the boom sticks kept all the wood straight in line so that it was easier to tow to town approximately twenty-five miles down river. This was how most log booms were made up north at the time. It was cheaper to transport these booms down the coast via the water.

I had gotten pretty good at booming these log bundles. So good, in fact, that Norman let me run the Windsor Creek operation. After I proved myself for a bit he even let me hire a friend or two to help on my little crew. I only really just needed one other guy to make this work, but it was cool to work with friends and get some responsibility under my belt.

The one thing I remember as a constant that fall was the rain and wind. It ended up being a stormy year. Every day it seemed we had to fight the cold and wet. We would struggle mightily some days. Summer booming was easy. The days were much longer and it was usually sunny and the conditions were calmer. That fall, however, was less than ideal. We had got through the fall and it was early December when Norman came to me and thanked me for the work I had done. We were all wrapped up in Windsor Creek and wouldn't be going back until the late spring. That meant I may not have much work for a bit as he had other guys working other spots and I was lower on the totem pole.

Norman, however, surprised me when he asked me if I would be interested in working a few extra weeks for a heli-logging crew he was going to set up near a little native village called Port Simpson. I was excited at the prospect of extra cash, so I said yes straight away. Then Norman paused and asked me if I was going to be returning to Vancouver to pursue my aviation career.

I had been wrestling with whether to go back to Vancouver or not for a few months, but this was the first time someone had confronted me on this decision. My mom and dad had kept quiet about it, occasionally asking where my thoughts were, but I think they must have been afraid that if they asked me too much I would say no just to spite them pushing me.

I had to tell Norman the truth. I wasn't planning on going back just yet. He, of course, talked to me about following my dreams and not letting my parents or myself down, but he eventually got to the point that I could continue to work for him if I kept working hard. He even mentioned that I seemed to have an ability to pick things up very quickly and he was impressed with my work ethic.

What if I had listened to my parents and Norman and went back to my aviation career? What if indeed?

Chapter Fourteen
Helicopter Logging and the Third Worst Decision of my Career

It was two weeks before Christmas in 1991 and I was going to work my first heli-logging show. I had been exposed to heli-logging working for Norman a few times. On a few occasions I would get put on the hillside to work beside the heli hookers. That term doesn't quite tell the whole truth.

The heli-hookers were the crew that hooked the logs up to the 150-foot-long mainline that the helicopter had secured underneath it. These big Sikorsky helicopters would fly to the hooker and they would communicate with two-way radios, using an imaginary clock and meters to guide the helicopter in. The guys would use the clock as a guide, saying, "I am at your two o'clock and three hundred meters," or about 980 feet. That would tell the pilots where to look on the mountainside for the guys wearing high-visibility hardhats and vests so they were easier to see.

This dance would play on all day. The guys working the hillside would have bundles of ten chokers all wrapped together. The bundles were dropped by a smaller helicopter at certain spots on the hillside, and they would hook the rope chokers around the logs. What a job. These guys were always in great shape because they ran all day and pulled rope chokers up hillsides.

I got dropped into this mess once or twice to help out. It was nerve-wracking stuff. Imagine this massive helicopter hovering above your head, pushing down huge forces of wind and blowing shit everywhere. The sound was deafening. You can't hear a thing, and you have to run underneath the helicopter, grab that long line, and hook a couple of logs to the hook and then get the hell out of the way as fast as possible while the helicopter tried to pull that weight to the landing drop area.

So when Norman proposed that I get involved in a heli-log operation, I was pretty excited. From my take this was a move up. So we gathered the gear over a few days and transported everything we needed to Port Simpson.

We did our company version of a pre-job plan and pre-job risk analysis. I was going to be in charge of the water drop area. Not quite what I saw coming, but it was still good because it meant I would be working longer than everyone else. As the young, aggressive guy in the group, the crew decided that I could handle the meetings and dictation and data entry. (The real reason was that I was one of a few guys who was literate.)

There were ten guys on this crew. Some were made up from Norman's company, such as the choker men on the hill working under the helicopter. Other crew were employed by the land owner to ensure quality control and so on. We all worked together the day before the logging was to begin, came up with risks that we needed to mitigate, put plans together, and the next day at seven in the morning we would all transport over to the job site.

We set up a large set of boom sticks in a giant circle on the water just off the north side of the island. The helicopter was going to pull the logs off the island right next to us and drop them in the circle, while I would operate a small boat and go to each turn as it was dropped into the water. I'd get the chokers off and re-bundle them for the smaller chopper to take them to the hill crew. It was going to be tough to keep up, but I felt up to the challenge.

However, we decided against better judgment to go to work when the weather was terrible and the waves were rolling in causing havoc with everything. The winds were gusting and the rain was coming down hard. We should have known better.

I remember the pre-job meeting like it was yesterday. The helicopter pilots were sitting with all of us listening to both the coast guard forecast and the aviation weather reports from Digby airport some twenty-five miles away that the winds were gusting to fifty kilometers (about thirty miles) and that the weather might break later in the morning. I sat there and listened to conversations about the risks involved with going to work. Norman was there, too, listening and making comments here and there. A native-owned logging company was paying for this work, and their head guy was there and he was of course pushing everyone to go. There was no money made when the helicopter didn't fly. Here was my first exposure to the heads of companies with different agendas having at each other.

I heard comments from the guy paying all the bills for the native band about how this was costing him ten thousand dollars an hour while we all sat there and debated. He said that they had flown in worse and nobody got hurt. So there it is ... because it hasn't happened yet, it must mean it never will. What a load of horseshit. We decided to go and start the work. I remember the ride out to the island in the tugboats. Waves were coming over the top of the bow of the boat and the crew was all sitting quietly. It was as if everyone knew someone was going to get hurt. The rain was pelting the windows of the boat.

We got to the site and it took an hour to prepare properly and then we got started. The wind hadn't really let up, but it was pretty constant at about thirty mile per hour. The waves beside the island weren't huge, only three or four feet, but they were rolling. The island was out in the middle of a large channel and it was blocking the lee side of the island from the bigger waves. Everything that got dropped into our circle of boom sticks was going to be climbing all over each other. We got about one hour into the work (which means the helicopter had dropped approximately thirty logs into the water) when the helicopter finished the first cycle and had to go for fuel. I needed the break. I was way behind retrieving the chokers off the logs. The guys in the hills needed more chokers, and I couldn't get them off the logs and wrapped back up and to the support helicopter fast enough.

The weather hadn't gotten worse, but I couldn't keep up. Every time I moved my boat into a position to retrieve a choker, the wind pushed me away and I had to reposition. People were on the radio telling me I needed to hurry up, and the pressure was getting to me. I started barking back on the radio. Guys got quiet. As I sat there trying to catch up while the wind and rain whipped across my face, and the boat I was operating pitched up and down in the increasingly rough seas, a voice I didn't need to hear comes on the radio and tells me to, "Get your ass moving and get those chokers onto the heli barge."

It was Norman. Shit. I didn't need that. I was sitting there, contemplating what to do. I couldn't go faster. Or could I? If I started walking out onto the logs instead of trying to get the chokers off the back of the boat, then I would cut down my times. I was weighing this all in my head when I heard the big chopper throttling up over on shore. This meant in two minutes he'd be right on top of me, and I couldn't get the guys their chokers. I wondered what getting fired would look like. I decided to make the third worst decision (you will learn about the first and second worst decisions later in this book) of my life.

I walked off the back of the boat and onto the logs, which were thrashing up and down in the waves. The wind was blowing saltwater into my eyes and the rain was whipping into my face. I could hardly see. Holy shit, I was cold. I started rolling the dice and walked farther and farther away from the boat. Success! I was getting to more and more of the chokers and was starting to clear the logs of all the back pile when the big Sikorsky returns with its first turn.

There was my personal gamble with the four cornerstones of business. I was willing, through my own actions or behaviors, to put the production cornerstone and the money and the time cornerstone ahead of the safety, health, and environment cornerstone. For me, the importance of getting production up reinforced my decision. I decided to perform at-risk behavior. I was making a personal choice to prioritize the money, production, and time cornerstones. The reasons for this were due to the stress (whether real or perceived) that I envisioned resulting from not getting production to a point that satisfied Norman.

Norman was production driven, and it amazes me how what interests leadership will fascinate the employees, and I was no different in this case. I chose to put myself at risk in the workplace, using my own behaviors to satisfy what I thought was an importance on production. I based my job security on it. There would be less stress to me if I managed to get production up to a point where Norman felt comfortable.

Guys were saying "Great job!" and "Nice work!" over the radio. It feels good when we hear that from our coworkers. It is called feedback, remember? Feedback is great when it's positive, but positive feedback to an individual can be dangerous if it drives us to behave at risk. While I was out on those logs rolling around in the ocean being abused by mother nature, I was being positively reinforced for my wrong behavior.

Remember the ABC model I wrote about earlier? I didn't know the science behind my actions on that day, but as I look back now it is pretty clear. The positive consequence of being applauded by my coworkers for my dangerous actions was reinforcing my desire to keep putting myself at risk. The four cornerstones of business were forefront in my decision making this day. I was balancing money, production, and time. The most important box of HSE wasn't even in my thinking that day.

I was putting myself at great personal risk while walking on those logs rolling in a mild storm. But I did not recognize that while I was performing the task—I wish I had. As the day went on for another hour or so, the weather got a little bit worse. The wind picked up and the waves started to get higher and it was harder and harder to walk those logs in the rolling seas. Here was where I learned about consequences for my behavior.

As I was starting to fall behind again and the conditions worsened, I got on the radio to Norm and said I could not keep up. I told him that the weather was slowing me down a lot and that I was scared. He came back over the radio and told me to do my best and he agreed that the conditions were not good. He told me over the radio he was checking with the client to discuss whether we were shutting down or not.

Saying the conditions were not good was an understatement. Saltwater stings your eyes when it blows into them and temporarily blinds you. I could not afford to be blinded in these circumstances. Try to balance yourself on logs rolling in the sea when you can't see. It is very dangerous. So dangerous, in fact, that people commonly lose their balance. They fall into the water, get crushed by the logs, and drown. Guess what happened next?

As I was trying to reach for a choker off a log that was rolling, I lost my vision for a second when the wind whipped saltwater into my eyes. I lost my balance and fell into the water. I couldn't see, because my first reaction was to open my eyes wide to get a bearing on where I was, and that completely blinded me. The next reaction when I hit the water was to take a big breath. I came up from the water, couldn't see, and gasped for air. I took in a mouthful of seawater as a wave rolled over me. So I was pretty much blind, couldn't breathe, and am panicking badly because the water is freezing and I can't find anything to grab onto.

That was the most scared I have been in my entire life. I was struggling in the water. I can swim like a fish in calm water, but not this. My work boots filled up with water as I thrashed around, trying to find a log to grasp onto. All my work gear got heavy with water, and I could feel myself beginning to sink below the waves.

I was so cold and scared. My vision was still not there. I could hear the helicopter coming into the boom with another load of logs. Did they know I was in the water? What if they dropped this turn right on top of me? Holy shit. I could hear the roar of the helicopter. I was starting to make out images as my vision came back. I had a few seconds to make the right decision. I could feel the weight of the water trying to pull me down. I could see something almost right in front of me. About two feet away I saw a log, floating in the water.

I couldn't get to it because my work boots were now full of water, and it was near impossible to kick my legs. My heavy work gear was making it difficult to tread water, and I was still partially blinded. I desperately grasped for the log in front of me … it was my lifeline. I needed it to survive. I lunged as best I could, my hand slapped it with tremendous force, and I clutched onto the log for dear life. I managed to get my body up to the log, and I was relieved and still scared, but joyous that I had the sort of life raft to hold onto. Just as I was thinking I had the situation partially in control, my plight went from bad to worse.

As the seas continue to roll, I got smashed into a log behind me while I was holding onto the one in front of me. All I heard was a cracking sound that I would later find out was my first of a few cracked or broken ribs. As much as that hurt, I was not letting go, even though it was now impossible to breathe. The pain was terrible. I was floating while clinging to a log that kept smashing me into another one. *Fuck me, this hurts*, I thought. I could see that the helicopter must have seen me, because it dropped its load and just hovered there, watching me. I found out later that they were thinking of dropping me the hook, but were afraid they would hit me in the head with it and knock me out.

I kept getting smacked into the logs. *My god I am going to die* was all I could think. As far as I knew, no one could get to me quickly, so I seriously began to think I was going to die. It took only a millisecond to come to that disturbing reality. A lot of things run through your head when this real situation presents itself.

Just when I thought I couldn't hold on any more, I noticed that the boat was a few feet from me. It had drifted back to me. That was my first good luck of the day. It was right in front of me, so with every last bit of my strength I lunged for it, and fell short by a couple of feet. I couldn't move my arms very well and the pain in my ribs was terrible. I tried again, and lunged forward, dragging myself across the mess of logs that continued to heave in the waves. I made it to the side of the boat. I couldn't stand up, so I just lunged one more time and fell over the side of the boat.

I was lying at the bottom of my skiff in terrible pain. I could see the big helicopter over me. The pilot, who was 150 feet above me, stared down through the glass bubble window and gave me a thumbs-up signal while hovering. The radio on my chest wasn't working. Funny how electronics and water don't go well together. I was so sore, so cold. I broke down into tears. That was too close. I didn't even have the strength to lean over the boat and wave for help to the other support boats. They must have seen this. I was lying there, crying, scared stiff, and then I heard someone call my name.

The voice was getting closer. I couldn't yell back, I was too sore. I could hardly breathe. Finally, I heard the voice again and it is within a few feet. I looked up and it was Norman. He ran across the logs in these terrible conditions to get to me. As I was lying there, he jumped into the boat beside me, took my hand, and wrapped his arms around me and repeated over and over, "I am so sorry."

Chapter Fifteen
Conversations From
a Hospital Bed

I was flown to the Prince Rupert hospital in the same helicopter that just minutes before was dropping logs into the boom ground out in a storm. We landed at the Prince Rupert hospital and I got into the emergency room, got X-rays, and was treated for hypothermia. I spent two nights in the regional hospital. I remember my parents coming up and sitting with me and asking me if I was alright. In truth, I don't remember how bad the pain was. I only remember two things. It was very close to Christmas, and a children's choir came in singing to hospital patients. A girl who I didn't recognize must have known me somehow, and she turned to me as the singers left the room and said, "Merry Christmas, Dwayne." The other thing I remember is Norman coming to visit.

I was sitting there in the darkness of my hospital room, trying to not think about the day. Every time I did I felt sick. I don't know how to describe it, but the pain was tolerable and the thoughts were not. If memory serves my correctly, I believe I broke or cracked nine ribs that day. I was on some mild painkillers and was sitting there feeling very emotional. My parents had just left after they were sure I was okay, and they promised to be back in the morning with decent food. It was after visiting hours, so I figured it was going to be a long night of reflection, when I heard a shuffle behind the curtain separating my bed from the others.

It is quiet in hospitals at night, especially close to Christmas. Everyone is out at parties and going to dinners and families are preparing for the big events. It wasn't too hard to hear someone walking into the room at 10 pm when no one else is around. I looked to my left and saw Norman. He was standing there, just staring at me. I asked how long he had been there, and he replied with a sigh, "Not long enough." I was confused by his answer. It was not really what I was expecting. As I was trying to figure out how he got past security, I realized he was probably there to fire me. After all, I had done what I wasn't supposed to. I left the safety of the boat to walk the logs and I got pinched rolling the dice.

I was sure he could see the embarrassment on my face. I didn't even want to make eye contact with him, because I was worried I would break down. I didn't want that twice in one day. I had cried in front of him earlier that day, that was one time too many. All I could muster was that I was sorry. When those words left my mouth, I was sure he could see the tear roll down my cheek. The silence was too much. I looked over and locked eyes with Norman. He was glaring at me with disbelief.

"You are sorry? Dwayne, you have nothing to be sorry about!" he said. I was confused, and not by the drugs, either. I didn't know why he said that. In my mind, I didn't do my job. I failed to keep up with the helicopter crews and ultimately I cost him and everyone else money by getting hurt. As I was lying there, he put his hand on my shoulder and said, "I did this to you. You were doing what I told you to do." He stopped talking for a minute, just looking into my eyes. Then glanced at my ribs all bandaged up and said, "You don't deserve to be here in this bed banged up the way you are. I should be lying there."

As I sat there listening to Norman's voice, I could tell he was struggling to keep it together. He was in pain. Not the pain like I was in. In many ways, his pain was much worse. He told me that night that he pushed me to do what I did and that the guys on the radio did the same as him. He let money influence his decision, putting me at risk, and he was ashamed of his decision. He further went on to tell me that he had met with my mom and apologized to her. That couldn't have been easy. He told her why I did what I did, explaining the circumstances influencing my decisions.

Norm then went on to tell me that the entire crew met that day at the shop and they discussed what had happened. They were all sorry. They would all contact me to apologize. I was dumfounded. This was not what I expected. I look back and think of that moment fondly. What is interesting about it is I have never told anyone until now about the conversation that Norman and I had in the hospital that night. Some things you shout out to the world, others you keep locked away. I share it in this book to give a man credit when it is due. Many people would not have looked into the mirror to ask what was influencing a worker's decision. Norman looked into the mirror deep and long and he did not like what was looking back.

I was of course off work for a few months. I had to heal ribs that were not so willing to heal. This was when I started working out and going to the local health clubs. I wanted to be stronger than ever when it was time to go back to work. Originally, I was supposed to get back to my flight career, but when I got hurt all that seemed lost for a bit. A lot of energy went into getting healthy. Breaking ribs sucks. So many times we can rehab a bad knee or a bad back, but broken ribs are a beast of a different feather.

Four months went by, and I got the all clear to go back to work from the doctor. I had spent a lot of time working out, trying to get my upper body strength to a better level. I wasn't going to get broken again, not if I could help it. Norman and I kept talking while I was recovering, and he had to reassure me after every conversation that I still had a job. As I went back to work, he asked me about when I was going to go back to Vancouver, and I told him I wasn't planning on it right yet. Not working for a bit had hit the bank account a bit. Worker's compensation paid me for awhile, but not as much as I was used to making, and when you aren't going to work every day you find stupid things to spend money on.

It was the spring of 1992, and Norman had a logging show that was going on down the coast for a smaller broker. This job would work out nicely as it would fit into the work schedule as a job we could do for a few months before the booming work began again up the Skeena River at Windsor Creek. Once Windsor Creek started, Norm had a new contract to work an area called Alpha Bay, approximately thirty-five miles south from Prince Rupert on Pitt Island. It was shaping up to be a busy year.

Norman had told me if I was serious about sticking around, he could use me for a couple of important roles. I have to tell you, though, that after the day lying in the back of the boat staring up at the wet sky, I wondered if I even wanted to return to the logging industry. If I had made such a decision, it would make my parents very happy, but in my quest to become a young man I had come to the determination that this would probably be the best route for me at this point in my life.

In truth, and in retrospect, I wonder if I was afraid to actually go and start my aviation career.

When I look back and wonder, did I stay behind and start working full time in the logging industry so that I didn't have to actually start becoming an adult? I am not even really sure I have the right answer to this question. The fact that I can look back on it and wonder probably shows me the correct answer. As long as I can remember, my dream was to fly, or be the passenger in an airplane. When actually confronted with my new career, perhaps I wasn't ready. It wasn't as if logging was any easier, but I did have many years exposure to it, so it became natural for me in many respects. Give the boy a few summers in the bush, and he will begin to think that perhaps this is his new path to walk.

So after I spoke to Norman, and he made it clear that he had full-time work as long as I wanted it, I began to realize that this could be a great opportunity for me. I decided to take him up on his offer, and his reward to me was the role of supervisor. Now I don't want anyone thinking that this meant I was all of a sudden in charge of a very large logging operation. It meant that I would be a supervisor in many of the smaller divisions that made up Norman's large company.

My very first glamorous experience as a supervisor was that of chief boom man. Before you go and think that I moved up fast, I want to make it clear that I was in charge of one person ... me. Yup, that is correct. I got the title of chief boom man by basically being my own boss. As we were heading south of Prince Rupert down the Grenville Channel to one of the inner islands to work on a small block of timber, I got to hold the title of chief boom man, which once again meant that I was going to be on that very same boat that had almost drowned beside a few months earlier.

When I look back, I think I understand what Norman was trying to accomplish. He wanted me to confront my fears around the water. I wasn't terrified of the water or anything along those lines, but I was nervous as hell. I will admit that. I was qualified to perform a bunch of different jobs at this particular logging show. I can't deny it, though, anyone who ever worked with me commented on how natural I was on the water. Whether it was booming log bundles, or flat rafting logs, or towing booms around the coast, I apparently had a knack for it, Don't know where the knack came from, though.

Although I did not really want to work the water, I realize today that I was the best qualified, and it meant tackling my fears and also helping Norman. I still felt I owed him that. The logging down there was beautiful. It was mid-spring on the coast. The weather was unseasonably warm (which meant high teens or low twenties). It was sunny all the time, it seemed. We were down there, logging for a few months, getting all the wood prepared for the big ship that would come to take all this wood somewhere around the world. I never did ask where some of these log ships were going. I had been told China, Japan, Korea, and Australia where the common destinations.

As I watched the log ship load up with a month and a half's worth of logs, I remember sitting with a guy who was the operations manager for heli logging company we had been working with for one and half months now. His name was Graham. Graham was a guy everyone respected. He was way too young to be in charge of all these guys, I thought. I got to know him pretty good over that month and a half. I was by far the youngest guy in camp at twenty-one years old. He was twenty-nine. Everyone else was in their late thirties or early forties. So we would talk here and there. He had built up his reputation through hard work and dedication.

He had a young family back home, which meant a wife and child. I was always amazed how much the guys respected him. The other thing I wondered was how he had risen up so fast in this industry. It wasn't common to see guys his age as the boss. He told me that he actually owned the company we were working with. Okay, that was unexpected. All I could ask was, "How?" He explained that he took a couple of chances and got the right contract and the rest fell into place. This guy was cool, and rich for a guy his age . All that ran through my mind was, "Could I do the same thing he was doing?" Why not? I could work like he did and build a company up, sell it, and retire at thirty from the real world and go back to aviation with a boatload of money. This will be easy … wrong.

Graham ended up offering me a job. He flat-out told me that I had a good work ethic, and he wanted me to work with his helicopter hill crews as a choker man. This would mean I could work on the hillsides of the mountains underneath the helicopter hooking up the logs. This was always something I wanted to pursue. The guys that did this type of hooking were considered gods in the industry. This was dangerous work and the guys who did it were paid big money. The lowest-paid guys would get 450 dollars a day to hook under the helicopter for nine hours. Guys who were in charge of the show could make up to 750 dollars a day. Keep in mind this was back in 1992.

So why do you think these guys made so much money? It was called danger pay. Anyone who worked a hillside underneath a helicopter earned every dollar of that money. The stress that these guys were under on a constant basis was indescribable. These guys ran around all day, up or down a mountainside, usually dragging a bundle or two of ten chokers, which aren't exactly light. Once the helicopter came to them for their "turn" of wood, they had to get out of Dodge as fast as possible, because time is money.

I was all fired up. I wanted to make that money and work alongside the hill gods (so to speak). There was a problem, though. I worked for Norman and he took a chance on me and I had to respect that before making any stupid decisions. Graham and his crew were leaving to go to work somewhere else and he gave me his number and told me to call him in a week or so. I had every intention of doing this. I had to stay behind to do clean up work and get all our gear ready for the tow to Alpha Bay.

This log camp was going to Alpha Bay, and once installed there I was going back to Windsor Creek on the Skeena River to boom for a few more months, and then that work would all be done. Busy year planned. During my finishing and clean-up work down the coast, I got some real good time alone with Norman. I told him about Graham, and was probably talking too much about him when Norman turned to me and said, "Dwayne, did Graham offer you a job?"

The first thought that entered my mind was that I really needed to talk less. He figured me out. Now that I had tipped my hat, I might as well fess up. "Yes," was all I could muster. Norman smiled a knowing grin and didn't say anything else. He didn't say anything for a long time. The whole time he was going about his business and I was going about mine, I was thinking he was going to ask any second if I was going to take the job. That didn't quite happen. The silence was killing me. I wanted to ask Norman his thoughts, but he didn't seem one bit concerned.

Maybe I wasn't as important as I thought to Norm's success. Maybe I wasn't really that good at my job. Then again, maybe he was sitting there figuring out how to kill me and bury the body. I was going to be spending the next three days with Norman towing the camp barge and the boom sticks the seventy miles or so north along the Grenville

Channel to Alpha Bay where our next job was. It was going to be just the two of us on Kaien Pride during this tow. The thing about log tows is that they take a long time. Even with a big tugboat that has lots of power, they don't go that fast. We were going to be towing all this heavy equipment, which didn't always tow well, and we had to go with the tides otherwise we would just burn fuel.

It was interesting how many lessons on business I was learning by working for Norman. Often I didn't realize what I had learned until I would go to make a decision later in my career, and I would remember my times working for Norman. These lessons on business influenced my decisions as an oilfield production manager years later. How to spend money the proper way, cash flow, inventory purchases, wage control, and morale issues were all things that needed dealing with on a regular basis. I remember those lessons. I carry them around still and they influence my decisions. My greatest take-away from working at T/R Contracting was the issues surrounding leadership and safety. I didn't make the connection in my brain until much later in life, sadly.

Chapter Sixteen
What's Fair in the Workplace

Norman and I spoke on the tow together, of course. Two days on the Kaien Pride towing, and then one day setting up the camp and dropping anchors and such gives a lot of time to discuss things. Norman already had this figured out. As an impatient twenty-one year old, I didn't have the patience or intelligence at this point in my life to let this happen. So we had our conversations about me being interested in Graham's offer and Norman handled it all well. He never jumped to any conclusions and listened as I sorted this dilemma out in my head. I finally come to the decision that I would be best served if I stayed with Norman, and I felt good about this decision. I was playing the part of smart ass too much, maybe. I mean, if Graham wanted me to work for him, and Norman also wanted me, perhaps I should ask for a little wage increase?

I knew that compared to a lot of the guys who worked for Norman, I was on the lower end of the pay scale. I got compensated fairly, don't get me wrong. But as a twenty-one year old, of course I figured I should be making the top wage. I worked harder than everyone else (so I thought), but it didn't mean that I worked smarter, and that was a key that I didn't yet understand. So I launched a little missile into the air to see if Norm would bite. Nothing happened. I was trying to get him to agree to pay me a buck more an hour. No dice. He wouldn't bite. I got a little impatient and start talking of other offers, when I really only had one offer from Graham. I was trying to show my considerable negotiating skills against a man who negotiated every day. Good luck to me.

I explained to Norman that I worked harder than everyone else and that I never said no to anything he asked. He agreed. He would have agreed with everyone who said they work hard. Imagine a guy telling you how hard they work and you saying, "No, you just work okay." That wouldn't be good. His negotiation would be done right there. So as I went on and on about how valuable I was, Norman let me in on a little secret. It would not be fair for him to give me what I wanted when there were other guys that worked as hard, not harder (nice choice of words Norman) than me. They had worked with him longer and he would be giving preferential treatment to me and he would not do that.

So I didn't get a raise. It sure didn't seem fair when Norm said no. He didn't just leave it there, however. He did go onto explain that as I had worked for him, I had gotten raises each year. He was right. I never asked for any raises until now. Each year, without issue, I would get a cost-of-living raise, and then an increase based on one more year working with Norman. He had even given me the increases when I was just a summer student. He didn't have to, it was good business and it kept his company known as an employer that people wanted to work for. There was a life lesson and a pretty significant business lesson as well.

If you look deep into almost any successful employer, large or small, this is a common thread. Being fair is good business. I will put it like this to make it perfectly clear.

I ask this question all the time when I work with groups on motivation. "How many people have left a great job because they saw preferential treatment and felt it was unfair?" If I am working with a group of thirty, usually 75 percent of the hands go up. Sometimes it's 100 percent. It is rarely less than 75 percent, though. I have never seen anything less than 50 percent. So as I developed my own series of questions that I used during motivation work, I came up with this.

"How many of us have hated a job, but stayed because of the people we worked with?" Usually 75 percent of the hands go up. Then I ask this follow-up question. "How many of us liked the job, maybe even loved the job, but left because we didn't like the leader?" I usually see almost every hand go up.

Norman gave me my first insight into this paradigm way back in 1992. Logging was tough. It was no walk in the park. The job was very physical, the work very dangerous, the conditions were often terrible, the hours were stupidly long. So if it was all these things, why did I love it so much? I can't answer that clearly other than to say, "I loved the people I worked with." What a cast of characters, you couldn't imagine a crazier ensemble.

Recovering drug addicts, recovering alcoholics, some current substances abusers, divorced people, single people, family men, and any other kind of person you could imagine. Some of these guys were absolute life fuck ups, but they were outstanding equipment operators or hill rats. It was sadly amazing to see a guy who could gamble away a paycheck in five minutes operate specialized equipment with ease. I didn't hate my job, but I didn't really love the job; I loved the people. It was the people, and the biggest reason of all was Norman. That man could make you feel so small at times, but he could also make you feel as if you could do anything.

He had us all convinced he could walk on water. One time during one of his legendary anger explosions, he was out on a log boom with a worker I never understood why Norm put up with. Let's call this guy Wilfred. Wilfred was a great person, always talking and laughing, and he was always smiling. The problem was he would smile all the time and there were times we needed to focus. So Wilfred was running this little winder tugboat, moving helicopter-dropped wood around. He was falling behind … badly. He just kept smiling and working at a snail's pace, and Norman was starting to turn a different color.

When we couldn't get the wood out of the way of the helicopter, it meant that they had to slow down or look for a hole to drop the wood into, and that cost time. Time was money in helicopter logging. It was essential to get the wood off the mountain as fast as possible. By falling behind we could cost the company a lot of money. So Wilfred was really behind, and he was just smiling away and talking to other guys on the radio. Norman was about ready to burst. He was out on one of his tugboats (he always liked to play around with the tugboats), and he had his radio on, listening to the work conversations. So imagine how freaked out he got when he heard the helicopter pilots begging for more space, and Wilfred isn't giving it to them.

Eventually, the chopper pilots called it quits and landed early to get refuelled, and this did not go over well. Norman had been working with one of his tugboats all day, moving large circles of bagged logs down the inlet a ways to provide more room for the helicopters to drop wood in the water. Now with the recent events of the helicopter landing, he made a beeline for Wilfred in his tug boat. Wilfred just kept working at a snail's pace. I was watching the distance between the two close, and

I was thinking aloud to the guy I was working with that this wasn't going to be good.

The guy agreed, and so I tried to go over in another boat to help Wilfred. I got to Wilfred just before just before Norm, and I told him that we should hurry. He just smiled and said, "Can't move any faster. I am not going to get hurt like you did." Holy shit. Those guys all still remembered my almost drowning. That was probably a really good thing. Maybe we all learned a lesson from that. Norm was now on top of us and he got real bad. He started barking at Wilfred, and Wilfred just kept smiling. Norman was getting madder as each second passed. Wilfred seemed to show little concern, so Norman finally said, "Are you even listening to me?"

Wilfred calmly said, "Yes." Norman then asked if he was going to get the lead out. Wilfred said he couldn't move any faster, and Norman came up with this gem. "Of course not, moving faster would mean that you were working." Wilfred just stared at Norman and a frown came to his face. His eyes began squint a bit, and his breathing got deeper. Wilfred tipped his head a bit downward. As I was watching this, I could clearly see anger blossoming on Wilfred's face. Please remember that I had not seen anyone confront Norman in almost five years working with him. I never would have expected Wilfred to be that guy who finally did it. Wilfred was so laid back, it just seemed out of character. I learn two valuable lessons then.

Wilfred yelled back with the precise clarity of a surgeon. His voice was at a perfect level, almost growling yet very clear. His eyes narrowed even further, and he was leaning as far over as he could without falling into the water. Wilfred and Norman were separated by about twenty feet of open water. It seemed like inches as Wilfred began to speak, "If you think I am gonna kill myself so you can make an extra fifty bucks, you are out of your mind." As Wilfred finished his statement, I turned my head slightly to watch Norman's reaction. I really did not want to be in the middle of this exchange, but I had nowhere to hide. Norman's face went blank for a second. His forehead began to wrinkle. I remember the sunlight making his grey-blue eyes look like ice. He looked like he was about to explode. His head was going to launch right off of his shoulders in a second.

Norman was getting ready to speak when Wilfred piped up again. "Dwayne almost got killed six months ago from this sort of shit. I can't swim underwater, remember that. You should know this better than anyone, Norman." And then Wilfred turned away and got back into his chair on his little boat, and proceeded to leave me drifting in my boat and Norman standing on the bridge of the Wee McKay tugboat. Norman and I didn't say a word. I just kept staring at the water. I was sure Norman was going to explode, and I worried it would be on me because I was the closest. Norman finally spoke. "Wilfred is right, Dwayne."

That was all he said. Not a word more. He still looked mad, but his tone was that of concern, not anger. As I looked up to see what Norman looked like, his back was already to me. He walked the few feet to the wheel of the tug, and I couldn't see his face. Not another word was said, and he slowly steered the boat back to his other duties. Funny thing was, Wilfred had everything cleaned up in a few minutes and we were back on track. All we lost was a little time that afternoon. Nothing more, and we of course gained that back as the day went on. I wanted to ask Wilfred about the exchange, but I also wanted to give him some time to calm down. I figured I owed him that.

Later in the day I got with Wilfred during the helicopter refuelling and asked him what he meant by saying, "You should know this better than anyone, Norman," comment. Wilfred kept his head down, staring at his coffee cup. He looked up at me very calmly and said, "Ask Norm." I figured Wilfred meant my accident from a few months back, so I just offered it out there and he sat quietly for an awkward few seconds and said again to ask Norman. This was actually causing me some grief. I wanted to know for sure whether that was what he meant or not. Why the darkness, why the BS? "What's the deal, Wilf?"

He just sat there and again said, "Ask Norman. You really need to ask him."

I realized that he wasn't going to tell me. I wanted to tell Wilfred that I was impressed as all hell that he stood up to Norman, but when I started to say something, he stopped me mid-sentence. He looked almost angry again but he had a grin on his face. "Dwayne, I have more respect for that man than I could possibly describe. Norman knows I am not the fastest or the smartest guy here. He lets me work for him and I know there are other people who can do what I do better. I didn't stand up to Norm to impress anyone. I did it so that he doesn't make the same mistake he did years ago. I care about him too much for that."

What the hell was he talking about? He knew something I needed to know. As I sat in dazed confusion, I looked at Wilfred. His grin was now a frown. He got up to go back to his boat. As he walked by me, he says this as well, "I was scared shitless that Norman was going to walk across the water and grab me by the neck." I laughed and Wilfred chuckled. It was a good tension breaker.

I wanted to make it more humorous by saying something smart as well, so I came up with, "Only Jesus could walk on water," and laughed some more.

Wilfred was chuckling, too, and it surprised me when his face went from smiling to dead serious and he came back with, "I'll bet Norman could walk on water if he was mad enough."

The first big lesson I pulled from that day's events was firstly to learn from your mistakes. Mine was to put myself at risk again to get a job done. It was only six short months since my near drowning and I had let slip my standards. Wilfred would not let his slip, and he was smarter than me for sticking to his guns. Part of my problem was my age as well. As young men, we are too willing to put ourselves at risk for the pure entertainment of it. Never mind putting ourselves in harm's way for work. We'll do it on purpose as young, adrenaline-seeking young men. Before anyone freaks out, it's not the young man's fault. It is all about brain development, or lack of it. There have been thousands of studies done by thousands of psychologists surrounding the frontal lobe of the brain and the cerebral cortex. The ten cent version is that the young male brain fails to develop until the mid twenties. At this point, the brain then begins to recognize the risk versus reward equation. Just think of the things we did as young males for entertainment.

We would drive too fast, go dirt biking, go fishing or hunting, jump off cliffs into small ponds of water, parachute, and bungee jump, all of this while drinking a beer or two or more. So because of Wilfred's experiences in life, he knew the consequences of taking such risks. His brain was more developed than mine and he was much more mature. The other big takeaway (remember, I said there were two) was that when confronted with a decision over doing it safely or doing it at-risk, doing it safely was the way to go. I will admit that I was afraid to confront Norman back on the day I had my accident. Maybe if I was more mature, I would have pushed back appropriately and Norman would have listened, and I would have never had the accident.

Never sacrifice yourself for work. Doing work right should not mean getting hurt or dying while doing it. This is a lesson that I never grasped until much later. Sadly.

Chapter Seventeen
Learning to Lead

As I worked my way through another year of logging, I found myself enjoying the challenges. It was hard work, but I was in tremendous shape. In logging you are always carrying something heavy or pulling something through the bush. A man's cardio gets to be pretty good when he's moving all day. I had to go for a doctor's appointment just before the summer of 1993, and I had decided to walk to the clinic and then up the stairs. When I climbed the stairs to the clinic, I had to have my heart rate taken. As I stood there, the nurse said it couldn't be correct, and she put the blood pressure cuff on me, which also measures heartbeats per minute. It came out at fifty-three. I had just walked the stairs and to the hospital. The nurse figured it was wrong because of how low it was. She tried it again and it was near fifty.

She then looked me and down and asked, "How good of shape are you in?" with a smile. I told her pretty good, and she said I was either a logger or a marathon runner. That should give you an idea of the shape you could get in while logging. I was also working out in the gym a lot. So much so that I developed a real passion for it, and I used to carry weight equipment with me when in the different logging camps, as well as a punching bag. I still have a punching bag to this day and lift weights as regularly as my travel schedule allows. Amazing what happens once we develop habits.

In the eighteen months since my water accident, I had developed some pretty good habits and some pretty bad ones. I became better at my tasks, had figured out how to do almost every job we had, and for the most part worked pretty safe. I still struggled with the knowing when it was the right time to not work based on safety issues. I always wanted to get-r-done. Far too often I would accomplish a task that someone else would think couldn't be done.

Of course I would get rewarded for accomplishing the impossible with an "atta boy" and a "job well done" and so on. This only further reinforced me to do what I shouldn't be doing. I began to develop bad habits. Because I could always get the job done, I would roll dice on the most dangerous of tasks. I talked about habit creation a couple of paragraphs ago. The brain initially takes in data and decides what it keeps, and the rest of that data is dropped, kicked out so to speak. Think of a time in your life when you wanted to know what time it was and you looked at your watch, got the time, and put your hand down. Then two seconds goes by and someone ask you for the time. What do we do? We have to look at our watch again. That's a classic example of how the brain takes in data, uses it, decides what it is going to store, and then dumps the rest.

Interestingly enough, it is actually a conscious decision that we make as to what we want to store in long term memory or not. Looking at the watch, getting the time, and then losing it almost immediately is an example of short-term memory. The time from the watch we looked at won't help us later on in the day, so we make the decision right after to dump that info. Workers do the same thing with data we give in the workplace. Data or direction is given to us, and we decide what to store or not to store. Based on the importance someone in authority places on regulations or policies we decide to store that in long term memory.

From here, though, we can't just leave thoughts or data in the long-term memory back to draw on anytime. We still have to reflect on the data, policy, or procedure in order to keep in the long-term memory bank. Think of phones numbers from a time before cell phones. We could remember hundreds of numbers, usually because we called them frequently. We didn't want to look up the same phone number a hundred times so we trained our brains to store the numbers in long-term memory. We make this decision consciously.

We create habits in the workplace in the same way. Why is it that we train people over and over again to ensure they do it right? We want to create a habit. If we do enough of a task the right way and consistently do it at least twenty-eight times, usually we will create a habit. If we keep doing it properly we will create a good habit. What happens, however, when we create a bad habit? It continues. The workplace is riddled with this sort of thing. We create a good habit and then allow a degradation of that habit and now the working habit is the one being practiced and now we are at risk. Dangerous stuff.

So I had some good habits and some bad ones. The good habits were usually the jobs we didn't do that much or tasks that required a lot of thought or planning. Where I used to get into trouble was the routine tasks. This is the usual workplace trend. It is usually the common tasks where workers cut corners. We become tolerant of the risk we see every day. I was no exception. The common injures we used to see logging were the old standbys that seem to apply to most every industry: slips, trips and falls. Not to mention cuts, bruises, scrapes, and hand injuries ... lots of hand injuries.

So there I am doing these dangerous jobs, and I am a danger to myself and everyone I work with.

I had gradually moved up through the ranks in this company to a point where I was leading men on certain crews. I had acquired some knowledge and skill around my work. There was always more to learn, but I was getting more responsibility all the time and Norman allowed me to branch out and try new things in his company. Our company had bid on some work up that Skeena River between Prince Rupert and Terrace, and this was exciting because it meant the crew could drive to work every day. No need for a camp at this site. For a young guy at twenty-two years old, this was heaven. I could be home every night. I would be able to see my friends, get a golf game in. Maybe take the girlfriend out on a date. Yeah right.

A move in a company means more responsibility. So when we would get back to town around 6:30 at night and everyone else was going home for dinner to do whatever it was they wanted to do, I usually had to fuel up the crew van, get chainsaw parts for the next day, or tune them up. I planned who was going to be doing what the next day and so on. The reality of the situation was the boat ride across the river and the fifty-minute drive home cost me time to do my required work. I was home at nights but not really home at nights, if you get my drift.

I have to tell you something else that I learned really quick when a company runs operations that bring men home every night. Sometimes men don't exactly act like men. We started having real issues with the same couple of guys not showing up for work each morning. We used to use the crew van (which sat fifteen people) to pick everyone up in the morning. Most of the guys had cars and they just met us at the shop each morning at 6 a.m.. We did have a few guys who didn't have vehicles or they left them with their wives or girlfriends, and we picked them up each morning. An interesting trend that I saw from this morning exercise as well, was that the guys who didn't have their own vehicles were the ones who used to get into the van stinking of last night's booze. These same guys slept the entire drive to the river boat.

You can see where I am going with this. These guys usually didn't have cars because whatever money they had was used to feed their addictions. These guys were never allowed on the hill if they were drunk, but they were sometimes hung over, which is just as dangerous. I should clarify, too, that these couple of guys weren't always getting into the van hung over. It usually occurred about as frequently as they got their paychecks. We usually got paid every two weeks, so when paydays rolled around, we could be sure a couple of guys were not going to show up.

The things we come to understand as we grow up. I talked to Norman on one particular day about a fella named Terry who was always late, stinking of booze, and just plain dangerous. Terry was the main guy in the ring of guys who either showed up really hung over or just didn't show up at all. This sort of behavior was particularly frustrating when each morning at 5:45 we would sit in front of Terry's house and he would either stagger out to the van or just not show at all. Frustrated guys would take turns getting out of the van and pounding his door in some mornings, and he would still not come out. What would usually happen on a day when Terry didn't show was Norman would phone me and say Terry talked to him and it was a domestic dispute, and we'd give him another chance and so he would get one. It was all just bullshit.

This guy in particular was the only one on the crew with industrial first aid. With a crew our size working the distance we did from a main medical center, it was mandatory that an employee on the crew had industrial first aid training. Terry was that guy for this company. These sorts of positions were usually filled by people who didn't have any other logging skills, so they would sit in the makeshift ambulance and read all day. Terry was different. He had good skills and realized it, and did his first aid duties and worked the landing (where the logs get pulled into) as a bucker-man (chain saw operator).

Terry's ability to do the two jobs simultaneously meant he was saving the company money (kind of). Norman was a business man, so Terry got more chances than he really deserved. When I got promoted (so to speak) to run the crew out at Alder Creek, it was a big deal for me. I wasn't going to allow these issues with Terry and others to continue. I explained to Norman that by allowing Terry back every time, he was actually making this problem worse. This was a tough sell to a tough man.

Norman was used to making his decisions and people following them. This was causing me grief as I started to run this crew. I already had enough issues to deal with as a young supervisor, or whatever my title was, and putting up with grown forty-year-old men who couldn't show any responsibility was the last thing I needed to worry about.

I had production numbers to get out, staffing concerns to worry about, and equipment that needed to be properly maintained. Guys like Terry were taking my energies in directions that were unproductive. So when I finally called a crew meeting to discuss with everyone the new expectations, I thought maybe Terry and a couple others would understand it meant them and they'd tow the line. Man, was I wrong.

I held the meeting and outlined just a couple of requirements. One was to be ready for work each day that we worked. The other was to be in proper working shape every day that we were scheduled to work. No exceptions. I had this meeting with the crew on a payday Friday, which meant that the entire crew would have two days off. Monday morning would be our first day back to work. I had nine guys all standing before me agreeing that they would be ready to go every day. A couple of very responsible workers came to me afterwards and commented that this speech was needed. One gentleman in particular said this to me, "Be prepared for a fight on your hands Monday morning with a couple of these guys." I wondered for a second if this fella was going to be one of the challenges, but I quickly thought about his work ethic and the responsibility he had always showed to his work, and I realized he probably wasn't going to be an issue.

I wanted to reach out a little more, and so I asked if he thought my talk was fair, and he said, "Yes." He also said it was about time. As my cohort walked away for the weekend, he turned with a smile and said again, "Be prepared for Monday."

Chapter Eighteen
The Problems with People and Rewards

I worried about Monday morning all weekend. I kept running through what I would have to do if a few guys didn't show up. What would I do? I only had enough guys to run the crew, and I typically needed about twelve to fourteen guys to safely and properly do the tower logging work. Four guys on the hill, one in the landing, me operating the log loader, one operating the tower yarder, three logging truck drivers, one boom man putting the wood into the log booms on the river, and one bucker in the landing that worked with the other loader operator. If I had tree fallers on the next cut block, I would have three or four others to manage as well.

If I had a road crew building a road, there would be at least four other workers also—lots to manage. My biggest fear was that our landing bucker, Terry, would not show up because he had the industrial first aid ticket we needed by law to ensure we were in compliance with provincial regulations.

Terry was a hard worker but he was one of those guys who had offsite issues. He drank a little too much, which is a kind way of saying he was pretty much a drunk. Terry was an intelligent person, he just didn't utilize his intelligence. He could have been a doctor if he wanted, but his social drinking had turned into a problem ten years prior, and as young man I was watching him deteriorate each year he worked for Norman.

My weekend was uneventful, even though I was thinking of Monday morning over and over again. I had the talk with the crew and most seemed to think it was about time. There were a few guys who had silly little grins on their faces, and when Monday morning arrived my worst fear was realized.

We sat out front of Terry's house for fifteen minutes in the work van. The crew boss went and banged on the door and eventually got Terry to answer it. He was still drunk. The guys in the van were all snickering and saying some pretty bad things about Terry when he got in the van. I watched everyone's reaction to him. Everyone was disgusted. He was so drunk he could hardly walk. I realized I had a tough decision on my hands.

I had told the guys to be ready for work, and here was one of my guys not fit for duty. I was being challenged right there. I looked to the gentleman who had told me to be ready for Monday, and here's what I did, much to the surprise of many on the van.

I looked at Terry very calmly, smiled, and asked him to get out of the van. He looked at me with a surprised look, snickered, and said, "Yeah, right." I sat back down and told the guys we couldn't go to work with Terry because he was in no condition to work. Almost in unison everyone agreed and told Terry to get out of the van. He sat there, defiant.

I smiled again and said, "Terry, you are not fit for duty and I will not jeopardize your health or anyone else's on this crew by placing their life in your hands." As our medic, he would be required to administer lifesaving first aid if anyone got hurt.

The guys all agreed. Many were getting pissed off, because we were starting to run late. Terry sat there and indignantly declared, "You can't run this crew today with my industrial first aid ticket, so either get going or I'll get out and report you to the Worker's Compensation Board and the Forestry Service for violating the regulations."

He was right, I needed him, but I didn't need him badly enough to put anyone at risk. I kept my cool, smiled, and said, "Terry, do what you must. I need you off this van right away. I have to go pick up our new medic on our way out of town."

It was like cannon fire going off. Terry looked at me and his attitude completely changed. I had reckoned with the warning on Friday from a very smart and helpful employee that Terry would be an issue Monday morning, so I spent Saturday making calls to friends in the industry and my dad helped me find a backup medic. I kept it quiet. I had hired him already but told no one other than Norman.

Terry then declared, "You can't just take my job away."

I looked at him seriously and said, "I didn't do anything to your job—you did." I continued, "Terry. You go sleep off the day and be ready for tomorrow morning at 5:35 a.m., not a minute later. Tomorrow we will go to work with you as part of the crew. Today will be recorded as a warning and go on file, but tomorrow is a fresh day. How's that sound?"

Terry looked around the van, and the faces on the people looking back at him told him to go to bed and be ready for tomorrow. He quietly got up and mumbled something about phoning Norman as he shut the door and myself and the rest of my supportive crew went to work and had a good day.

I wasn't completely surprised when Norman pulled me aside later that day and informed me Terry had called him at 6 a.m..

Norman asked me how it went with the new guy. The new guy was a WIP (Work in Progress) but he was young, not addicted to anything yet, had an industrial first aid ticket and was willing to learn. Norman smiled back and said, "Good, let's see what happens to Terry tomorrow and we'll go from there." Norman asked if I thought Terry would be ready. I didn't think he would. I didn't believe that Terry could just kick his drinking in one day. I explained this and Norman said he thought he would be ready and sober.

Norman asked me why I was so sure Terry would do the same thing tomorrow. My answer was simple yet complicated, and I had to be careful how I delivered it. Norman always had a tremendous faith in people. Guys like Terry had taken advantage of guys like Norman for a long time. I felt Norman was too easy on Terry and a few others because of his personal feelings. I explained to Norman that Terry didn't think anything would really happen. He thought he could just call Norman up, cry or whine or whatever you want to call it, and that all would be forgotten.

Norman struggled with my explanation. He said that his believing in people and giving second and third chances was why he had succeeded. My take was different based on reading a few books and articles on leadership and motivation. If I had let Terry just go with the status quo, he would have been positively reinforced for a negative behavior. Terry's behavior may have felt good for him, but not many others.

In fact, the negative was occurring. The motivated people on my crew were becoming unmotivated, because they saw the same thing happening over and over again and the end result not changing. I needed to change this. On a crew of twelve or fourteen guys, one person can negatively influence the others. I needed to send a clear message and be fair about it at the same time.

I had the talk with the crew on Friday, and they were waiting to see what was going to happen on Monday. If I hadn't followed through, my leadership would have been questioned, and people would not give me the 100 percent I needed to excel. I was a very young leader in this company, and I needed to get this right or I wouldn't be a leader for long.

Norman raised an eyebrow, cracked a smile, and said, "We'll know tomorrow, won't we?" As the day came to a close and the crew was driving back to town, several guys asked if we were going to pick up Terry in the morning.

I said, "Of course. If Terry is ready, he will be welcomed back." I wondered whether he was going to be ready the next morning. As the last guy got out of the van—the same gentleman who told me to be ready for Monday morning—smiled at me and said, "Nice work today. I think you just might make it."

Chapter Nineteen
The Next Morning

It was 5:34 a.m.. We were waiting in front of Terry's house. The lights were off, and there was no sign of life inside. All the guys were staring at his kitchen window. The clock turned to 5:35 a.m. on the van radio, no Terry. Everyone was looking at me. The van driver looked at me and asked what to do. I sat quietly for an extra three minutes, looking around the van. No one said anything. It was very quiet.

I look around at the staring faces and said, "What do you think, team?"

Almost in unison, everyone said, "Let's get going." We pulled away.

It was quieter than usual on the drive up. All day everyone worked hard, and no one spoke of the situation until the van ride home that night. Once close to town, a friend of Terry's on the crew spoke and said he had talked to Terry the night before and Terry said he was going to transfer to a different crew of Norman's. I didn't respond. I just sat there, and tried to show no emotion. Terry had decided to play his cards a little differently than I expected. He was going to Norman again for another chance.

The funny thing was that I had talked to Norman on the phone from the worksite earlier in the day and he had made no mention of it. So I was wondering who was in the dark here. I dropped the last guy off and started my journey to the company warehouse. As I pulled up, there was Terry talking to Norman.

I parked the van and got my gear, then went inside the warehouse. I plugged in the radios and got some equipment ready for the next day, when Norman and Terry came up to me. I just smiled at them both and asked what was up. Norman looked at me and said he was giving Terry a chance on a different crew. One more cannon blast delivered by Terry to me.

Of course I was furious, and I couldn't hide it. Terry had this little smirk on his face, like a little kid. I looked at Norman and asked him when this was decided. He looked puzzled at my question, and pissed that I would challenge him.

"Just now," he said.

"Jim told me fifteen minutes ago that you had already told Terry he could move onto another crew last night," I replied angrily. "So was the conversation today? Or was it last night?" Norman looked pissed off. One of his eyebrows lowered and his teeth began to appear from behind a snarl. Just when I thought I was going to get a blast from Norm, he spun around to Terry and asked if he had told Jim this.

Terry was visibly uncomfortable as he stammered out, "Yes."

Norman let out some language that I can't possibly in good faith write down. Norman was a man's man—if you lied to him, look out. Terry had been screwing around. He wasn't playing fair, he was acting like a child, and he was taking advantage of Norman ... and me.

Norman changed his mind on the spot and told Terry the only way he would ever work for him was through Dwayne's crew. He told Terry, "If you want a job, you can only have it with him," and Norman pointed to me.

Terry lowered his head and began to cry. He blurted out, "I have a drinking problem. I am trying to turn my life around."

Norman called bullshit and became even more angry, saying, "People who turn their lives around show up for work, and they take their situation seriously. You have issues, and until you go and get them resolved, you are done here in this company."

Then Norman turned to me and said, "You don't have to be here for the rest of this discussion. I will call you later." That was my signal to get the hell out. So I did, and didn't see Terry for about two months. I am glad I did see him again, because he became very important to me.

Chapter Twenty
How Did I Get Here?

Imagine, if you will, waking from a very long sleep. You know what I am talking about. We have all had those nights when we went to bed so tired we could hardly pull the sheets back. Whether it was because we had days, or for some of us, weeks, without proper rest. The sleep I am describing is the one we wake up from and we actually feel as if we are drunk or hung over ... or worse yet, we feel like we have not slept at all.

As we come out of unconsciousness, our heads are throbbing and our bodies ache. As far as I am concerned, this is one of the worst feelings we could have. Maybe it's the alarm ringing, or you hear the sound an annoying disc jockey bantering on the radio, but when we wake from this night's sleep we usually feel worse than when we went to bed.

So we lie there for a few minutes trying to figure out why we feel the way we do. I tend to sleep on my back just before I wake, so when I come out of these sleeps I end up looking to the ceiling with blurred vision. I stare at the pattern in the ceiling above me as I slowly begin to absorb my surroundings. I may notice the trickle of light coming through the blinds indicating morning has begun. Possibly the sound of birds chirping outside brings me serenity.

On this morning in particular I woke from my sleep and found it increasingly hard to focus. I have woken up before feeling this way. Not that often, but often enough that I recognized how the morning would play out. When I have had these bad sleeps, I find my day is almost always a struggle. Thoughts don't go together as they normally would and any physical activity ends up with some sort of bruised knee or strained hand. I didn't hear the peaceful symphony of the birds and the trickles of light didn't seem to be coming from the window in my room.

As I further came out of the fog, I began to realize that my surroundings were not anything I had seen before. I was really groggy, but even being this groggy I could recognize that I was not in my bed at home. I heard the constant beep, beep, beep, beep of some electronic device near me. I didn't remember hearing this tone before. At first I thought it was my alarm clock, but it wasn't. This sound was quieter and had a second between each beep. My alarm clock never did that. It just lets out one loud and long and continuous squeal until I shut it off.

I tried to lift my head to look around, and I was petrified by the reality that I couldn't. I wanted to, but I couldn't. I couldn't seem to muster the strength to lift my head to survey my surroundings. I struggled to lift my arms in a desperate attempt to lift my body up in bed, but I couldn't do that either. I had no strength. This is when I realized that my body felt a way I had never felt before, which is that I couldn't really feel anything. What a trip. *I must have gotten really smashed last night, to have a headache of this magnitude and not be able to use my arms or lift my head. Another day of self-induced sickness, but wait a second … I don't drink that much.*

I sat there for a few seconds and tried to remember the wild night, but I drew a blank. I didn't remember going out with friends. In fact, I didn't remember much of anything. What did I do yesterday to feel this way? Where was I? How did I get there? As I pondered each of those questions, I tried to focus my vision. It was then I noticed that there was a person or persons beside me to my left. I couldn't really make them out, but I did recognize the voices.

One of those voices was my mom. I couldn't really see her, but I could make out her silhouette. Funny how I couldn't see her, but I could hear her. The other voice sounded like that of my family doctor. Why the hell would my doctor and my mom be hanging out in my apartment beside my bed? I still couldn't focus my vision and my body hurt more and more with every second as I began to regain some more consciousness.

Then I heard my mom's voice crack, and she said, "Dwayne, can you hear me?" I could hear her, and I could kind of see her, but not really yet. My eyes wouldn't focus. I couldn't get them to do what I wanted.

Fuck, this is a terrible headache. My head was pounding, I couldn't open my eyes properly, and I couldn't seem to use my arms or even lift my head. *What the hell did I drink last night?*

I could still hear that beep, beep, beep coming from somewhere near me. I didn't exactly know where that beeping was coming from, but it was getting a little faster. I was starting to get a little excited as I lay there. Why couldn't I focus? I heard Mom asking me again if I could hear her. I wanted to answer her so she'd stop asking, and so I could ask her some questions about this pickle I found myself in. I tried to answer her, but all I could get out as a response was, "Mmmmmm."

What the hell was that? I couldn't even speak? My mild amusement at not knowing where I was and why I couldn't seem to wake up was now replaced with fear. Seconds before I thought maybe I was hung over, now I was not even sure if I was really awake. Maybe I was dreaming? It didn't seem like a dream. More like a nightmare. I was pretty damn sure I was awake. My mom's voice cracked again and she repeated, "Can you hear me?" Of course I could, but my tongue and mouth didn't want to work.

I could hear the beeping getting a little faster. It sounded almost as one continuous tone, it was beeping so fast. I was starting to really freak out, and was trying to move around while lying there, but my body wasn't working as I remembered it should. I tried to move my head and it took few seconds to happen. I was really scared. What the hell was going on? I tried to call out to my mom, and I still could only muster a long moan. Mom was now standing right over me; she was practically on top of me. I could see her hand coming to touch my forehead. I could see that her hand should be on my scalp. I should be able to feel this.

She was saying something. I had to focus very hard to hear, as there were now other voices in the room. I noticed silhouettes on all sides of me. I couldn't really hear just Mom, the other voices were talking to each other from different points in the room. Mom was saying something, but I couldn't make it out. I was so confused! What the hell was going on? Mom was leaning right over me and I still couldn't make out her face. I knew it was her, though. Then I made out what she was saying, and it all started to come back me. She jogged my memory with one little statement and everything started to fall in place in a matter of seconds.

"You were in an accident, Dwayne!" And so that is where it began, and I started to remember those events that I had not remembered until just then when Mom's comment jogged my memory. With one little reminder, everything came flooding back to my conscious. I had been in accident. I did not at this point know how bad that accident was, because it rendered me unconscious. As I lay there on that bed, I began to realize exactly where I was.

The beeping I heard from beside me was the machine that measures your heart rate and keeps track of blood pressure. As I begin to notice what the sound was, I also noticed that it was beeping more rapidly. *This can't be good for me*, I thought, and although I still couldn't focus my vision enough to tell what my surroundings looked like, I did know that I was in a hospital bed. Those other people in the room with me and mom were doctors and nurses. They were doing some sort of work around me, although I couldn't really tell what that was.

I kept hearing Mom's voice. It was telling me to calm down. "Stop getting excited, everything is going to be okay." I remember hearing that more than once. Why do things need to be okay? How badly was I hurt? These were questions I wanted to ask, but I was too excited. That was the last thing I remembered until I woke up again several hours later.

Chapter Twenty-One
My Fall From a Mountain

Iwoke up three days after the accident, still resting in my hospital bed. My injuries were numerous, and they would take a while to heal. A lot longer than the usual things I used to have to recover from during my logging career. Bruised knees took a few days, twisted ankles and bloodied fingers all healed really quickly in comparison to what I was suffering from. In order to understand the extent of my injuries, we need to back up to how I got them.

I had been standing on the edge of a mountainside logging road in the Alder Creek logging operation. Alder Creek was the name given to this tributary of the Skeena River about halfway between Terrace and my hometown of Prince Rupert. This logging operation was along the south shore of the Skeena River. Alder Creek was only accessible from Highway 16 by travelling the fifty minutes or so on the highway and then taking a boat across the one and a half miles of river that separated the north and south shore.

This was where I had been running a crew of men for a few months now, and it was also where I had to fire Terry. Well, Norman fired him, but you get the meaning. Funnily enough, Terry was back working for Norman's company ... and me.

Terry had a conversation with Norman that night and he went to rehab. He worked his way through the process and was fit and healthy and quick-witted and back working on my crew. He was a delight, and he was a damn good medic. So good a medic, in fact, that he is the reason why I can write this book. I was in a terrible accident. I was in an avalanche, and Terry kept me alive. That's right ... Terry kept me alive.

I was trying to listen to my family doctor describe what was broken on me. The injuries were numerous, too many for me to comprehend all at once. I still hadn't quite pieced together exactly what had happened. But as the days went by, more blanks got filled in by different people coming to see me. Everyone provided me a little piece of the puzzle. In truth, there are still parts of that day that I don't remember.

In hindsight, it was probably best that I don't remember some of what went on. To recall some of the events may have been very damaging to how I went about the rest of life. Let me share with you what I remember, and what I also pieced together from witnesses. I have spent a lot of hours creating a timeline to ensure accuracy, as many of us know the truth sometimes gets lost in how we remember events. I have tried to be as accurate as I can in putting to paper what happened on the mountainside that late September day back in 1993.

I mentioned earlier that Prince Rupert is famous for two things, salmon fishing and rain. September of 1993 validated the reason why Prince Rupert was famous for rain. As Prince Rupert sits on the coast of the North Pacific it gets exposed to the wettest weather system known to man (kidding). It would rain sideways sometimes, and it would rain and rain and rain for weeks, not just days. This September was rare, not because it wasn't raining, but because it was raining too hard even for what Prince Rupert was used to.

I am describing rain falling ... big deal, right? That's what I thought at first when it just kept raining and raining, no big deal. We were used to working in these conditions, but what happens when someone logs all the trees off the side of a mountain? We had just spent about four months logging off twenty thousand meters (over 65,00 feet) of wood off the logging block. This meant that we had an area of one mile long by a quarter mile wide where we had removed every single tree. This logging scar was on the slope of a mountain valley. So if a logging company removes all the trees from the side of a mountain, it means that the trees that used to act as filters and gathering points for all this rain were gone, and that rain water would run down a mountainside without anything to suck up the moisture.

You get the picture I am painting. There it is, raining more than ever before, and the natural vegetation is gone, allowing the water to degrade the soil on these steep slopes. We built logging roads high up this cut block, and the rain water was coming down the mountain, pulling dirt and roots and anything else loose down the hillside. All of this debris was making its way down the mountain and ending up on this high logging road. There were culverts built into the road and proper ditching, but it was raining so hard that the ditches have backed up onto the road. The culverts can't let enough water out of them, because all of this debris from the logging made its way to the culverts and partially blocked them all off.

So now within a few hours we had an entire road flooding that was about two thousand feet above the river. The culvert pipes that ran under the road to let the water through to the slope of the mountain were blocked with bark, roots, branches, leaves, and broken tree parts. These trees parts were blocking the pipes and the road was become dangerous to travel on. The culvert pipes being blocked were causing a large ponds of water to back onto the road and it was flooding a long way back from the culverts.

The water was actually running over the road and falling off the other side. This wasn't good, as the water was actually degrading the road integrity. We had logging trucks running over this road every forty minutes or so. To have this road wash out or away could cause us big grief in maintaining our production. If the road became unstable, we would have to shut down for at least a day until the road-building excavators could make it to our site and repair the culvert.

We would commonly use two-way radios to communicate with each other on the mountainside. As the crew lead, I would have to talk with the logging truck drivers and rubber tired loader operators down on the landing where they would bundle and dump the wood.

One of the logging truck drivers called me up on the two way and indicated he was a little nervous about the condition of the road at the fork culvert. It had been raining hard for a few days and today it was especially wet. I told the truck driver that I would go and check it out and get back to him. So I shut my machine down (this day I was operating the big log loader that loaded the logging trucks) and headed down to the culvert about a half mile away in one of the company pickups.

I parked back far enough so that if the culvert did wash away, that the truck would be safe. As I got within a couple hundred feet, I could see why the logging truck guys were so worried. From two hundred feet back, I could see that almost 150 feet of the road was underwater. Not a lot of water, just a few inches on top of the road. That meant, however, that the side ditches of the road were also filled with water, and the pond that surrounded the culvert pipe was filled up as well.

The pond surrounding the culvert wasn't that deep, maybe ten feet at the deepest point, but as I walked toward the culvert it began to enter my mind that this once-small pond was actually quite large now, and the weight of all that water pushing against that area would be a lot more side-loading than that road was used to.

I got within about thirty feet of the center of the culvert, and I could see that the water was now running over the road, dropping off the other side, and running down the mountain. This water was not following the old creek bed that the culvert pipe assured would occur. Because the water was going to the path of least resistance, it meant that there was a lot of erosion happening on the drop-off side of the road. Please remember that these mountain logging roads were built onto steep grades, so there was a pretty substantial drop off of about twenty to twenty five feet on the other side of the road.

When this water dropped off the road, it fell with some force and quickly eroded the base of the logging road. I could actually see large chunks of earth rolling down the hill for quite some distance due to the steep grade. As I watched each second pass by and saw all of this erosion occurring before my eyes, it hit me that although this road might not wash out right then … it could. The safe thing to do—the responsible thing to do—would be to shut this road down.

So I made the call over the two-way radio device to the truckers, telling them that it was probably best if we shut the road down for the day. No sense risking anyone's well being up there. One of the truckers was almost to the top of the hill, so he would shortly be in sight, and he asked me the question that will forever haunt me, "What are the chances of that road giving away?" I was walking back to my pickup as that question came across the radio. I was grabbing pylons to lay out on the road so that no trucks would enter this area.

As I gathered the pylons and walked back and began to lay them straight across the road to ensure no one crossed, I answered back with, "The chances of this road giving out are probably one in one thousand."

The logging truck operator came back on the radio and said, "Good call." I was pleased with that response. It validated my rationale. A couple of other logging truck guys came on the radio and commented on my decision to shut the road down. Everyone supported it so far.

As I was standing there on the logging road in a downpour, basking in the glow of my managerial prowess, I walked one last time over to the culvert and took a look at the outlet side of the pipe. There was very little water actually making it through the culvert. The culvert pipe was two feet around. I couldn't see what was jamming the culvert, but based on the dark, muddy color of the water, I could say that I figured it was a lot of crap and debris. The water was dirty from all the sediment and soil washing off the mountain onto the road.

As I stood right there between the two sets of pylons, I watched a small mudslide come down the mountain about one hundred feet further down the road. This was a little mudslide, nothing too big. It was about a dump truck's full load of dirt that tumbled down the mountain and ended up on the logging road. Watching this little amount of dirt come down the mountain slope and slap hard into the road made me realize the energy that was stored in that little pile of dirt.

The dump-truck-sized load of dirt came crashing down the mountain and hit the road with great force and blew chunks of wood and mud and rock in all directions. I remember having to duck and turn as rocks came flying at me and splashed heavily into the water that was surrounding me. A couple of stumps came rolling down the hill and they crashed right onto the pile of dirt that had just come down, and then they bounced off the pile and flew across the road and went over the road. Then they crashed down the mountainside for another two hundred feet or so.

That really got me thinking. Those two stumps were probably about a thousand pounds each. These were massive stumps with roots that were toppling over themselves, bouncing ten and fifteen feet into the air. They looked like ugly basketballs as they bounced down the mountainside. Every time one of the stumps would hit the mountain and launch back into the air, a big chunk of dirt and debris would follow the stump down.

Watching this damage, I began to realize that this mountainside was in a more precarious position than I thought. The damage and instability of this mountain was greater than I estimated. I needed to get everyone away from this site quickly. I had already told the logging truck drivers to stay down at the bottom landing, but I still had a crew of workers working back where I had first come from. There were at least seven guys back about a half mile from me that were working with the big logging tower and running equipment. There were seven lives, plus mine, at risk. That wasn't sitting well with me.

I was working through the best possible way to get everyone off the mountain, and I was standing between the pylons I laid out about ten minutes ago. This was the original trouble area, and as I was standing there, figuring out the safest and best way to get everyone off the mountain, guess what happened? I knew better than to be standing where I was. I had just shut down the road because of the real fear I had that it would give way, and yet there I was, thinking I was bulletproof, even after I had nearly drowned in a storm months before. I was putting myself at risk. This is why I call this the second-worst decision in my life. I should have known better.

I heard at a loud crack just over my shoulder, and as I turned to look up the mountain I felt a rumble beneath my feet. I began to lose my balance a bit. I turned to look straight up the mountain, and then I heard a roar. As I struggled for my balance, the ground around me started to shake violently and I fell to my knees. As I stared up the mountain from my hands and knees, I saw a wall of darkness crashing toward me. I couldn't get up, because the ground around me was disappearing. I was falling into a hole, the culvert pipe and all the surrounding road was disappearing beneath me. In milliseconds I realized that the culvert and road was washing away.

I began to fall down the mountainside with all the water and mud and road material. I saw darkness coming at me at a high rate of speed. The mountain had given way at the culvert, and the road was gone. When that road washed out, the mountain slope from the culvert all the way straight up to the top of the mountain began to wash out, too. I was right in the middle of a mountain coming apart.

For the first three days after the accident, I only remembered about three minute's worth of time in one-minute sections.

The first minute I remember is waking up not long after the mountain came down on me. Of course I was not very lucid when I woke up from being knocked out, and as I was trying to figure out where I was, I remembered hearing loud noises, and then my vision started to come back. I never recalled what anyone looked like. It is a scary thing waking up and not understanding why there are people all over you. The loud noise was actually coming from the helicopter that I was in. I was being flown by air ambulance to Prince Rupert. I have no idea how long it took for the machine to get to us. I have no idea what my crew did to get me out of the mudslide I was in.

When the mudslide carried me down the mountain, I ended up rolling about one hundred feet, and I then got thrown out of the slide. I continued crashing and flipping head over heels with rocks, sticks, stumps, and other debris, and I came to rest on the mountain as the slide continued on past me. In the most amazing bit of luck that I have ever seen, I was partially protected by a huge stump that I fell into. The huge roots of the stump protected me from the tons of earth rushing past.

Terry, our medic, and the rest of the crew picked me off the mountain and transported me by pickup to the lower river landing where an air ambulance was called to pick me up. As I lay on the stretcher in the helicopter, I tried to look around me to see what was going on. For whatever reason I couldn't move my head very well. It seemed to be restricted for some reason. The most terrifying thing of all was although I knew I was banged up pretty good, I couldn't feel anything.

When I work with groups each week around North America, I often ask my people to bring the back of their hand up to their mouth and blow on it. I then ask, "What does that feel like?" People will share all sorts of sensations they feel. They can feel the warmth of their breath on the back of the hand, some even comment (male participants only) that they can feel the hairs on the back of the hand moving around. The next question I ask is, "Would you be scared if you knew someone was pushing against you and moving your arms and you couldn't feel it?"

People answer that one with an uneasy quiet and the answer is always, "Yes."

As I was lying on the stretcher, I was still trying to figure everything out. I had just woken up from unconsciousness and had no clue what had just happened to me. I couldn't feel anything and that had me frightened. I could see the paramedics working on me, but I still couldn't feel it. As I was trying to look around and get a better handle on the situation, I noticed I was having trouble breathing. I just couldn't get a deep breath in or exhale properly.

So, naturally, I wanted to look down at my chest to see if someone was putting pressure on it, and as I looked down I started to get the magnitude of my situation. There was something sticking out of my chest. Nothing too big, but something that definitely caught the eye. As I struggled to focus on what this object was, I could tell that there was a red, liquid-like substance on it and that it was sticking straight up and was about the size of a pen in length and diameter.

As I got my eyes to finally focus, I saw that there was a little stick piercing my chest. I can vividly remember staring at this little stick coming out of my chest, and wondering why I couldn't feel it. I had been hurt pretty good a couple of times in my life to this point, and remember saying that, "I never wanted to feel that way again." As I lay there in the back of the air ambulance, I wished like hell I could feel that stick. The worst thoughts ran through my mind. I couldn't feel and I couldn't move, so I began to think I was paralyzed.

That was a lot to grasp in one minute. It wasn't the best minute of my life. I started to listen what was being said around me, as opposed to what was going on around me, because I couldn't get my eyes to focus. I probably shouldn't have listened. The paramedics were talking about how much blood I might have lost, how I was in shock, how damaged my face was, and that we were flying really low because they thought I had a punctured lung, and then finally that my legs must be broken in several spots and probably my hips were broken.

As I heard that comment, I tried to look down and I still couldn't. Something was stopping me from moving my head. I was trying to look around, and out of the corner of my eye I saw my work boot. I had to focus so hard to actually see it. *Alright, excellent, I didn't lose a pair of work boots, good.* I was mildly happy with this knowledge when I started to notice that the boot had a foot in it and the leg was attached, but it was resting in a terrible position. My left leg was rolled over, it seemed. I did not remember being able to put my leg in that position. I was a flexible guy for twenty-two years old, but not that flexible. I passed out.

The second block of time I recall from that day is this. I am unsure how long I was out, but I awoke when the paramedics were taking me out of the back of the air ambulance and wheeling me through the Prince Rupert Regional Hospital. I had been unconscious for probably fifteen minutes, and I was still very groggy and unable to focus my eyes.

The paramedics were met at the helicopter by a doctor and a nurse, and they started wheeling me on the stretcher to emergency. As we entered emergency, I could see two figures standing beside the entrance. I couldn't focus my vision, but I was damn sure it was Mom and Dad. They gave off an energy that I recognized. When I was wheeled closer and could focus, I could tell both of them looked very upset and they were doing everything they could to put on brave faces.

I was used to Mom crying. Not that she went around crying all the time, but moms cry. When a sad movie was on television or someone we knew died, I remember mom crying. That's what moms do. So to see her on the verge of tears as they wheeled me past her on the way to emergency didn't really surprise me. To see my dad standing there was a shock, period. To see Dad looking like he was ready to cry really pushed me over the edge.

My dad was also in the logging industry, and he was always working at some logging camp somewhere. So to see Dad standing there with Mom confused me. To see Dad with that much concern in his eyes was the worst feeling in my short life. I didn't know how bad I looked, hell, I didn't even know what had happened. I must give perspective on seeing my dad this notably shaken up. My dad wasn't really a touchy feely guy. He was a great guy but he worked a lot.

When Dad was born in 1943 in New Westminster (a suburb of Vancouver). The doctors must have taken a look at him as a newborn and figured he wasn't quite ready for the real world. So my dad was given back to his parents (my nanny and papa) and they decided to take him into the wilderness and raise him in the forests of the Northwest Coast of British Columbia. Of course I am kidding about the doctor telling my nana and papa to take Dad out to the wilderness to raise him, but that's how Dad tells it.

My dad has told me numerous times that he was about eleven years old before the family moved to Prince Rupert from the various logging camps they lived in back in the 40s and 50s. Dad told me that many logging families would actually just move to the logging site out at the end of the world and stay there until the job was done. His family had a cabin-style home called a float camp that they towed all over the Skeena River to where the work was. My nana used to teach the other children in the logging camps their primary schooling.

Dad's brother and two sisters and every other family like them were the true pioneers of the Pacific Northwest. So if Dad was raised in a remote camp back in the 40s and 50s, how tough of a guy do you think he was? I don't mean fighting tough, I mean how strong physically do you think he was, and do you think Dad had a lot of emotions he shared with people? The answer is, of course, "No."

To put this further in perspective, I remember being about sixteen years old, chopping wood out behind our garage and piling it up before winter one year. I was working alongside Dad and it was a cold November morning. As I was chopping with the axe, my hands were getting really cold, so I did what anyone would, I put a pair of gloves on. I kept chopping for about ten minutes and dad had this perplexed look on his face as we worked side by side. Eventually he looked at me and said, "Take those gloves off, Dwayne,, men don't wear gloves when they work."

I wondered if this meant Dad had finally acknowledged that I was a man. So I looked up and asked, "This means I am a man, Dad?"

I said it more as question than a statement, and he looked over at me with a look of mild amusement and said, "Don't kid yourself," and reached over and grabbed my gloves and threw them over his shoulder into the dirt. That is the kind of man my dad was.

So when Dad was standing there at the entrance to the emergency room, and I could see fear in his eyes, I will say that I was more scared than at any time in my life. As I drifted into unconsciousness, I thought again, *what the hell did I do to myself?*

The third and last time I woke up for a while was when my family doctor was sitting beside me in the emergency room. I have been told that they kept taking X-rays, because my doctor and the emergency room doctor couldn't believe that I wasn't in worse condition considering what had happened. I was taken to a special room behind the emergency room, and this is where I remember the doctors and nurses looking over my body with confused looks on their faces.

My family doctor was going over every inch of my body and really paying a lot of attention down near my chest. He also kept going back to my legs, and working his way up to my head. He did this very slowly, at least twice. He would stop at a point on my body and say something to a nurse who would then write something down. I still couldn't focus my eyes very well, but I could hear things like, "His legs are going to be okay," and "He has little holes all over his chest." What kind of holes was he talking about?

Chapter Twenty-Two
My Tumble, My Injuries

No one saw me go down the mountain. One of the logging truck drivers came up the road to turn around and head back down to the lower landing, and he saw the mudslide covering the road. He noticed my pickup truck parked a hundred feet or so from the culvert that was now washed away. He tried to call me on the two-way radio and he didn't get an answer. This didn't worry him at first, but he decided to walk to the slide and see if I was there.

Once he got to where the road was washed out, he saw my hard hat just off to the side of the slide and that caused him some concern. He started calling out for me and I didn't answer, so he began to look up the road to see if I had walked back to the logging tower. He could see that my machine at the high landing wasn't operating, so he began to look for me around the mudslide more.

He had somehow gotten the attention of some of the other guys working up on the logging tower, and as they came to join him in looking for me, he saw my high-visibility vest poking through a tangled mess of wood and mud. Once he realized I was still wearing the vest, he ran down the slide the hundred or so feet to me and started throwing rocks and mud and sticks away from me to uncover the rest of my mostly-buried body.

I wrote earlier of a big old stump that I got tangled up in that probably saved my life. That couldn't be more true as it was described to me. When I got tangled into the stump and rolled down the mountain with the slide, that stump and its mass of roots kept me from being crushed and buried under the tons of mud and debris. When the stump then rolled out of the slide and came to rest beside the mudslide that continued on down the mountain for another five hundred to six hundred feet, I was kept safe.

When Ted got to me, he couldn't get me out from the stump roots on his own. The rest of the crew had now seen what was going on and they were rushing to help him. Once there were enough guys, they cut some of the root away with chainsaws and dug me out of the mud. Once I was out of the mud, they carried me down the mountain on a spine board to the bottom logging road. How they kept my two-hundred-plus pound frame secure while carrying me down the mountain through all that uneven steep ground amazes me. To all the boys from the hill crew who carried me down that mountain through the mud, rocks, stumps, sticks, and logging debris in that downpour ... thank you.

The hill crew then put me into the back of a pickup truck and drove the three miles to the bottom landing on a bouncy logging road to the first aid station (an old ambulance that was parked at the lower landing), where they awaited the arrival of the air ambulance. Alder Creek was about fifty miles from Prince Rupert by helicopter. Those guys managed to keep their heads after pulling me out of the mudslide and called the air ambulance, giving them directions as to how to get where we were. Then as they transported me to the bottom landing, Terry tried to keep me stable while waiting for the air ambulance. He held my hand and talked to me the whole time as if I were awake, never leaving my side.

During this time, many of the crew I worked with were looking at me and making their own determinations as to what was wrong with me. Terry was the only medically-trained EMT on the crew, and he was apparently very calm throughout (which was out of character), but he told one of the boys to phone my mom and let her know what had happened. I don't know who made the call, but whoever did was trying to give my mom the facts, and they weren't pretty. My mom was told over the phone that I had two broken legs, and that my chest was crushed and I had little puncture wounds all over me. Somewhere in these conversations Mom was told that I was probably not going to make it.

That explained her look in the emergency room. Not that mom wouldn't have been worried, but imagine as a parent getting the phone call all parents dread their entire life. The worst part of all for mom, as she explains it, was the waiting. When mom got the phone call from one of the guys on the crew it was within ten minutes of them getting me out of the slide. Mom knew where Alder Creek was, and she knew that even by helicopter it was going to be thirty minutes before the helicopter got a crew into it and prepared it properly, and then the flight time to Alder would be about thirty minutes.

Then I would have to be loaded into the helicopter, secured medically, and then flown to Prince Rupert. Mom told me that waiting at the hospital, going over and over in her mind what kind of shape I would show up in, was terrible. Mom was up there alone for almost two hours until my dad had somehow been notified and he rushed to the hospital to meet her. Dad had just lifted off in a seaplane to head to work at another logging camp when the pilot came over the radio and told dad that they were flying me to the hospital and they turned around and dropped Dad off. He got to the hospital minutes before I landed.

I remember Dr. McDonald sitting with me in the emergency room just before I passed out. This is third minute of time that I remember. I described it briefly a few paragraphs ago, but I want to share with you the last words I remember of that day. He was sitting beside me on a little rolling stool, and I was lying on the stretcher. I had an IV in, and the doctor was pulling debris and rocks and sticks out of my wounds. They didn't want to give me any painkillers because I had lost so much blood. A nurse was addressing something below my chest. There were people coming and going all around us, but I only focused on Dr. McDonald.

He had been my doctor since childbirth. That's one of the benefits of growing up in a small town. People that stay there usually want to stay there, and Dr. McDonald was no exception. He was such a kind and gentle man. As I lay there, he very gently leaned over, smiled (man, I needed to see that smile), and said this, "Dwayne, what have you done to yourself?" I smiled back weakly but couldn't answer. I didn't remember anything from my fall.

He saw my pain, and so he brought his head real close to mine and said in an almost-whisper, "I don't know what you have been doing with this body of yours, but it probably just saved your life. These next few days are going to be tough on you, Dwayne. I need you to hang in there, I need you to fight." That's all I remember of the rest of that day.

Chapter Twenty-Three
My Personal Experimentation with Health and Fitness

The reason Dr. McDonald said, "I don't know what you have been doing with this body of yours, but it probably saved your life," should definitely be expanded some more. I was in pretty good shape. I worked out in the local gym all the time and was always running around in logging camps doing very physical work. The ugly truth of the matter, though, was that about six months before I fell off the mountainside I began to experiment with steroids.

I took a cycle of pills called D-Ball, which was dianobol, a very popular steroid back in 1993. The first cycle I took was two hundred pills, and I got some pretty outrageous muscle gains from that first cycle. When I was done that first cycle, I waited the eight weeks required for the body to produce natural testosterone again, and decided to take five hundred pills of dianobol and one hundred milligrams of liquid testosterone enanthate. The cycle I just describe gave me even more outrageous muscle growth

To put the muscle growth in perspective, I can describe it like this. I have worked out with weights since I was about thirteen years old. As a teenager, I was always chunky. I could have lost a few pounds most of my teenage years. I really got into lifting weights when I started college. I lifted weights after school almost every day for three years, and read the books and took natural supplements. I got into really great shape.

I stayed pretty much the same weight—I would put on about five to seven pounds per year. When I started really lifting weights I was twenty years old and weighed about 160 pounds and was five foot, ten inches tall. As I mentioned, I grew slowly and put muscle on bit by bit. When I did my first cycle of steroids, however, I put on fifteen pounds in two months. That was a big change, and people noticed it. When I finished the first cycle of steroids, I kept about ten pounds of that first fifteen. I thought, "If I can put ten pounds on by doing a little cycle, what could I do with a big cycle?"

That was my rationale for doing five hundred pills of D-ball and one hundred milligrams of testosterone. I was correct thinking the bigger the cycle, the bigger the gains. I went from about 175 pounds to 185 pounds on the first cycle, and then from 185 pounds to 205 pounds on the second. Pretty significant body change. Although I thought I had everyone fooled around me, I didn't. Most people knew something was up, but would keep their comments to themselves. My parents asked me a few times but I convinced them I was using protein powders and so on.

I couldn't fool Dr. McDonald, however, and he called me on it right there in that emergency room. He did it in such a gentle way. He was probably right that being built the way I was saved my life. Tumbling down that mountain and getting wrapped up in a stump would have killed most people. No matter what I had put into my body that helped me survive the fall, my life changed that day. I was in for long road to recovery.

I woke up a couple of days later with a long list of injuries. I had suffered several broken ribs, a punctured lung, and numerous lacerations to the hands, arms, chest, and face. My upper body was covered in bruises, and I had numerous little puncture wounds all over my chest, back, and shoulders. My legs weren't broken as originally thought, but my left hip was damaged and my left knee was all torn up—the medial collateral ligament was damaged, as was the patellar tendon.

The little puncture wounds all over my upper body were in fact sticks and debris and rocks that had hit me so hard they dug little holes out of my skin. That is why I remember the little pen-like object sticking out just below my chest. I had a few of these little sticks that were hanging off of me. The sticks had pierced my skin just deep enough to get lodged into me, but not so deep that they caused much damage.

The stick I remember looking at just below my left chest was not responsible for the punctured lung. If I remember it correctly, that punctured lung was from one of the broken ribs. That stick in my chest was pretty mild compared to the one that was lodged into my left shoulder. The stick that went into my left shoulder had moved around a bit more in my upper shoulder area, and to this day I have a pretty significant scar along the top of my left shoulder.

My mom tells of the amazing yet sick story of me lying in bed while she and dad went over my body trying to figure out how many of these little holes there were on me. Mom described them to me as "little cigarette burns." They were everywhere. I was scalped a bit, too, when a chunk of something tore the skin away from my right forehead. I have very interesting scars along my eyebrows and forehead. Chicks dig scars, remember? The most interesting thing of all was that I didn't hit anything major. Luck was on my side, and who wants to rely on that?

And so for the second time in my young life I was lying in a hospital bed, wondering how I got there. I had told myself during my last recovery from almost drowning two years before that I would never put myself in the line of fire again, and there I was, all banged up because I did put myself in the line of fire. I sure didn't seem to learn my lesson.

Funny how we rationalize situations in our life and convince ourselves that *this time* it will be okay. One in a thousand my ass, try one in one. What the hell are the odds on that? Let me answer that for you ... 100 percent.

The third day after my roll down the mountain was when I started to remember things that happened to me. I remember my family coming to see me, my mom and dad and one of my brothers. My other brother was at Notre Dame academy in Saskatchewan, not the Note Dame in South Bend, Indiana. For Canadians, the Notre Dame in Wilcox is just as sacred an education as the American version, and the real reason we carry a passion for that school is it also produces some of the finest hockey players in Canada, and in Canada that is very important.

Wilcox to Prince Rupert was almost two thousand miles away, so Daryl phoned to see if I was okay. I even had an ex-girlfriend or two come visit me. It was nice to see friendly faces, but all I remember wanting to do was sleep. I was so banged up that anytime someone new would come to see me, they had to be prepared before they entered my hospital room. It wasn't pretty. All I wanted to do was sleep; that's the way our body recovers. It takes a lot of energy to heal from what I had been through. I would fall asleep for a few hours and then wake up when a nurse would come and ask the routine questions about pain and so on.

I woke from one of those sleeps at about 10:30 p.m. on the third night in the hospital to a familiar figure sitting in a chair at the foot of bed. It was Norman. For the second time he was in a room with me in a quiet hospital. As I began to focus on Norman and wake from my pains, he let out a crooked grin and a deep breath and said, "This is strangely familiar, isn't it?"

Through my yawns, I asked how he got through security again, and he looked back very seriously and said, "That isn't anything that you should worry about right now." Oh, shit. I could tell from his tone of voice and the seriousness of his gaze that this wasn't going to be a chat about the weather and how sorry he was that I did this to myself.

Amazing how fast I was able to clear my head and focus on the conversation. I went from sleeping to intense in about two seconds. Norman was glaring right through me. It was as if I wasn't what he was focusing on. There must have been something behind me that had his attention, because his stare seemed to go right through me. Hospitals are dark and very quiet at night. I wondered if anyone would hear me scream if he attacked me. That thought entered my mind.

We sat there staring at each other for about a minute. I could hear his deep breaths as he looked through me. After thirty seconds, his eyes turned to my body as I lay there. He went from my head to my feet with his eyes slowly looking over me. "These injuries are going to take longer than the last ones to heal," he said quietly. He looked at the floor in front of him. "Dwayne, how is it that you keep finding yourself in these situations?"

I contemplated the correct response. I remembered that my parents had taught me to give "logically well thought out answers," and as I was going to respond, I realized that I couldn't. I had no way to logically explain why I was again having a conversation while lying in a hospital bed. My drowning was explained by getting pushed to do a job in terrible conditions and not knowing how to push back.

The fall off the mountain—well, that wasn't logically explained. I started to panic. Norman wouldn't be asking that question this early in our talk if he wasn't upset and ready to take action. Action that would probably mean I wouldn't be working for him anymore. Could he fire me while I was in the hospital?

A million different thoughts were flying around in my head, and I finally rested on, "I don't know." I started to defend myself by saying, "I don't even remember what happened," and was getting ready to plead my case further when he stopped me mid-sentence by raising his hand slightly to his side and kind of gently waving it as if to say stop. Norman leaned forward in his chair, let out a very deep breath, locked eyes with me, and said, "I am not going to have you kill yourself working for me."

Nothing was said for a minute after he spoke. I sat there staring at him for ten seconds, and then I looked away. I was getting fired in the hospital. A tear started to roll down my cheek. *Great, I am going to cry in front of the toughest man I know. This will go over like a fart in church.* I looked around the room, wanting to look at anything but him. There was more than just one tear now. I found a tile on the floor to gaze at, and just sat there staring at it in the silence of the hospital.

If I looked at Norman, I was sure that I would start to bawl like a little baby, so I just stared at the floor and started to wonder what had gone wrong. As I began to drift into thoughts of my life and what my next step was, Norman broke the silence with a deeper breath and a shuffling in his chair. The shuffling caught my attention and I figured he did it to move in for the kill, so I looked up at him. I wanted to see this coming. If he couldn't tell seconds ago that I was crying, he absolutely knew now. I was starring right at him, both eyes leaking tears.

I must have looked pathetic! Norman looked at me for a moment, then got up out of the chair and went to a little night table beside my bed and got me a box of tissue paper. He handed it to me gently and told me to wipe my eyes. He must have not liked looking at them all wet from crying. As I blew my nose and wiped the tears away, he stood at the foot of my hospital bed, both hands on the foot rest. Norman then began to speak.

He was almost whispering as he said this, "Dwayne, I am not going to have you kill yourself while you work for me! I have been thinking about this long and hard, and I have decided that you are either going to take on the role of safety in my company and do that with every bit of conviction that you have shown on anything I have asked of you, or we are going to say goodbye to each other right here and right now."

Norman was looking through me again as he finished. It was the most intense moment I have ever had in my life. He looked so sadly serious. I was about to say something. I figured I should at least respond to his statement, so as I shifted in my bed to talk, he looked at me with an even greater seriousness and added, "This isn't negotiable, Dwayne. Think carefully before you say anything. I will not have your death on my shoulders. I am willing to put an end to our working relationship right here and right now unless you agree."

Okay, he had said twice in thirty seconds that he was willing to cut me loose. Norman wasn't the kind of man who liked to repeat himself. So when he said it again, I figured I was already walking a thin line. I had better give a response pretty quick. We locked eyes again, and his stare had no hint of letting up. His ice-blue eyes were piercing. I could hear him breathing heavily in the quiet of the hospital room.

I dropped my head and said, "Okay." I wasn't really keen on this idea. In the thirty seconds or so that I had to think it through, all I could think of was how on so many occasions the workers would comment about "safety crap," and "we could get more done around here if we had less of this safety stuff to deal with." The guys I was exposed to over the last few years had tried to work safely if it was rewarding to do so, but so often I saw guys do things that were risky, and they were rewarded for it with a "good job" or "I can't believe you pulled that off."

Safety seemed to be one of those things that people really weren't that passionate about unless the boss told them to. So to take on the safety stuff for the logging company really didn't appeal to me. I was boxed in, though, outflanked … again. I made a lot of money for a twenty-one year old. Hell, I made a lot of money, period. I was working about nine to ten months a year and making about seventy-five thousand to eighty thousand dollars a year. I didn't want to give that up.

That was the real reason I said yes. Before our talk was done, Norman added that he would help me whatever way he needed to, and he would continue to pay me while I recovered from my injuries. He would also pay for whatever training I needed. He also said I wasn't going to be changing my roles, he was just adding to them. So from here on out I was also going to have to work harder as my workload was being switched. It was growing, and that sucked.

Just what I needed … more work. I was already working twelve to fourteen hours per day. How was I going to fit safety responsibilities into all my other duties? I started to ask these questions in a flurry of speech. Norman told me to calm down as he finally started to show some emotion and cracked a little smile. He continued to smile a bit as he explained that he would be supporting me and that he wanted me to engage the entire workforce in helping me with safety. His comment was, "Safety is everyone's responsibility, and everyone needs to be involved." I couldn't wait for him to try that gem at the first safety meeting.

Chapter Twenty-Four
Safety Reality

When Norman came to me and we had our second late-night hospital chat, I told myself that I wasn't going to take those risks anymore. I figured I had gotten lucky and I had better learn from it or I may pay a higher price still. So after a few weeks of recovering and months still of healing, I went back to work on a limited basis and began to help out with the safety concerns of Norm's logging company. There had never been a "safety guy" so to speak, so this was going to be interesting.

I mentioned earlier that no single person carried the title of safety manager for Norman's company, and just because he told me that I was going to do this it didn't mean any fancy office or announcement. It meant that I was now supposed to help direct the safety initiatives in this company. I had known for a long time how we as a workforce had viewed safety issues.

When the Worker's Compensation Board (WCB) used to come out for inspections on worksites, we used to give those guys a pretty hard time. We would have fun at their expense and make jokes surrounding the reason why they were working for the WCB, like, "You must have not been able to cut it on the hillside," or "What happened, did you get hurt?" Now I was supposed to be involved, and all I could think of was, "Is that what the guys think of me?"

The reality of the situation was that almost all these individuals who would visit our worksites had a true passion for safety. These people would come out and help us, coach us, and try and motivate us to work safer. Our reaction to this was to feign interest or in some cases not show interest. When I look back, it was probably a lack of maturity on my part and also a lack of knowledge. I figured I had the answers as young man. What a shock, right? I was young in the workforce but my views were shaped from my experiences, and many of the older workers showed this same contempt.

It wasn't just that, though. There was a reason why we viewed these safety guys or gals this way. When I look back, I can say that about two-thirds of the people I was exposed to in safety roles were legitimately caring individuals who were trying their damnedest to get people to work safer. The other one third was what we commonly referred to as the "safety cop." A phrase that I learned from one of my leadership coworkers to describe these individuals was "safety knob."

The "safety knob," or "knobs," were the people who came out to site and quoted regulation and wrote everyone up and walked around with an iron fist. And even though these safety knobs accounted for only one third of what we were exposed to, they painted the entire profession with a brush that was not flattering. As soon as one of these safety knobs showed up, we as a workforce went into overdrive to shut them down. The workforce would try to work safe while these individuals were around, and these dorks would still get in people's faces and abuse the role of safety. The minute they left, the workforce went back to working the way they did before, and all that was discussed was the jackass that just left. No one would talk about how to work safe. They would actually talk about the opposite.

The "safety knob" was a character I did not want to become. So when I set out trying to change the workplace perspective on safety, I went out with the intention of getting the guys I worked with to *want* to work safe, instead of having to. There were days of great success, and those were usually the days when I went out with a plan of engagement. Instead of me telling them how to work safe, they told me. That was a trend that I recognized early on and tried to encourage on a daily basis.

Don't get me wrong. There were many days when I went out with the best intention of engaging the people I worked with, and fell into the trap of telling them what to do. Sometimes I would even get challenged with the old lines of, "You used to do this task this way, Dwayne!" Wow. Who knew people were watching what I was doing? My past would come back to haunt me several times.

It was the winter of 1994, and we were having our year-end wrap up party. Nothing too extravagant, just a few drinks with the boys from the company at the company shop and some finger foods. Everyone was there and we were sharing stories of the past year and talking about how we got the wood off the hills and what we could change going into next year. The guys were really letting loose and being honest. I had been performing my dual role as a guy involved in safety for the company and had some good success, and some noticeable failures.

As we were all talking this December day just before Christmas, I began to hear the guys actually talking about how they could see the change coming in the industry where safety and working safe were going to be mandatory. They were saying that *not* working safely would actually cost companies more than following the safety regulations. I found it interesting that the boys were having this conversation. I had never really pictured these guys sitting around talking about safety, but here they were in a social setting having a few beers and talking safety. Holy shit.

Chapter Twenty-Five
My Friend Terry

Not everyone was drinking alcohol at the Christmas party that year. Terry, the man I fired (with Norman's permission), the man Norman sent to rehab, the same Terry who remained sober and an excellent worksite EMT who saved my life when the avalanche crushed me, was the only man at the party not drinking.

Terry was listening to the conversations around safety and he waiting until everyone was off onto other conversations when he spoke to me. I could sense that Terry had something on his mind as he kind of hovered around and moved closer when everyone was out of earshot.

He smiled, wished me Merry Christmas, and asked how my wounds were healing. Terry and I had talked before about my day on the mountain, but there was more depth in this conversation than the previous ones, as we laughed about whether I was going to make it in the company. I was laughing pretty hard when I realized that I should thank Terry for keeping his head and providing me the care I needed. I was thinking that no matter what training I had, I would probably would have cracked under that strain.

I blurted out, "Thanks for keeping me around, Terry."

He looked at me and said, "Thanks for keeping me around, Dwayne." He reached over and hugged me. I could tell he was nervous and uncomfortable, and he began to cry and looked me straight in the eye and said, "If you hadn't let me back, I probably would have killed myself with the bottle."

What Terry meant by "If you hadn't let me back," was once Terry had finished rehab, the only spot he was allowed to work as per Norman's direction was for me, if I wanted him. I remember vividly the night

Norman phoned me and asked that I go to his home office. I met him there that night and he told me Terry was back from his treatment and that he wanted to come back to work.

Norman asked what I thought. This was sometimes mistaken for, "Tell me what I want to hear." Those not intuitive enough to read between the lines would eventually be told by Norman what to think.

When he posed that question to me, I tried a different response. "What do you think, Norman?" I asked.

He looked back as if I had slapped him. He actually shook his head as if to reset and starting smiling. He said, "You have learned much, my young apprentice," which was eerily similar to what Yoda said to Luke Skywalker about what he did and did not know in *Return of the Jedi*. I had decided to use the open-ended question tactic that I learned at one of my training classes. Close-ended questions get a yes or no. I needed to know Norman's point of view and see if it differed drastically from mine. If our views were similar, no problem, but if they weren't it would give an insight into his, and then how to counter.

Norman countered with, "My point of view doesn't matter when I ask one of my people for theirs."

Shit … shit … shit. Outflanked again, damn. To make a complicated story uncomplicated, I can just say this. Norman phoned Terry while we were together and Terry didn't know I was there, and Norman asked Terry what he had heard about the Alder Creek crew since he left a few months back.

Terry's response shocked me, made me proud, and got me a raise in pay all at once. Terry told Norman that all the guys liked the way things were going. That they had freedom to make the decisions and that I supported their decisions, and if they were the wrong ones I helped them find the right ones. "Dwayne lets them all be leaders," was Terry's exact quote.

Based on that conversation, I figured if Terry could tell Norman those things about me that I could at least give him a second chance. It must have been tough to say those things to Norman after I fired him.

Norman taught me about faith in humanity, through Terry, and I was rewarded with a medic who saved my life. I would like to think that Terry saved me as I saved him, and we were even. Merry Christmas, Terry. Merry Christmas and thank you.

Chapter Twenty-Six
85 Percent Committed

It was like a hammer hitting me on the head at the party that night. The crew was sharing in a relaxed atmosphere, and were generating some really good ideas. I had always figured these guys didn't really care about safety, but that was merely the perception, not the reality, and the perception was driving a big part of their behavior. How could I use all this horsepower and change the perception of this group of guys? We had already had pretty good success that year. The injuries were down by half and the company work hours had increased, so this was a good thing. We were statistically safer, but what did that mean?

The guys were talking about how they had taken a huge risk on a stand of timber by doing something called choker tagging. That was when you could hook a couple of chokers together (on a twenty-five foot wire) to get wood that was just out of reach of the mainline. You pull back on the mainline and lift simultaneously and free up heavy, trapped wood. The problem with this technique is that it pulls the nine guidelines in a lateral direction that the standing tower wasn't designed for. The risk is that the tower could fall over, and when that happened people were usually hurt, badly, or killed.

The guys would go from one story to another about how they rolled the dice, so to speak, and put themselves in harm's way to "get-r-done." Even though they all knew it was dangerous and that they would really rather not do these dangerous tasks, they based their actions on the perception that to *not* do it would be viewed as weakness. An entire crew knew how to work safe, but chose to work unsafe based on recognition. There was story after story about how risk was taken and how risk was rewarded.

No one sat around and said, "Yeah, remember when we worked really safely that day?" That was a conversation I never heard, not then and still not enough today. I hear it now, fifteen years later, but to change an entire workforce's perception is not easy. Look at how we have been rewarded almost our entire careers. "Get-r-done" was rewarded with more opportunity, which meant more money. I remember back twenty years ago when people weren't willing to take risks, they got fired.

We are patterned to accept risk, and we have a hard time breaking that pattern. I recognized sitting around and chatting with my friends and coworkers that I had my work cut out for me. This was going to be an interesting challenge. I have to admit when Norman told me I was going to start helping out with safety that I myself was in the "have to" state. I wanted to keep my job and it paid very well, so I was giving it a real effort, but if I had to gauge it, I would say I was 80 to 85 percent committed to the job assignment. Please remember that I still had my other responsibilities of running a crew, along with safety, so on some days it seemed overwhelming.

I thought eighty five percent was an achievement. If someone came to you today and said they needed you to keep doing your regular work but now you would also carry other duties, imagine how much trouble you would have juggling the requirement. I had trouble, too.

I remember talking to Norman the next day about my revelations at the Christmas gathering. It was the December 19, and the company was shutting down over the winter. We did this every year. The weather, and more importantly the amount of snow, was the main reason we broke up every year. The north coast of BC is famous for rain but it is also famous for snow in the winter time. South of Prince Rupert and toward the interior near Terrace it was not uncommon to have years where the valleys would accumulate ten feet of snow.

That much snow made getting to work very dangerous, and the logging roads were always at risk for snow slides and avalanches, so it made sense to shut down. We would also get the occasional cold weather snap, where temperatures would drop into the minus thirties for a stretch. That was too dangerous and risky to work in, so it was like a holiday every year from Christmas time to about mid to late March. By then, the warmer temperatures would have come and the snow would stop, and by mid April we could get back to logging.

This year wasn't going to be any different until I met with Norman, and he told me that a few of us were going to go down to work over the winter break doing some environmental cleanup on one of the projects we had just finished. Devon Lake was a large helicopter logging show we had finished on the southwest side of Pitt Island. It was about one hundred miles or so from Prince Rupert, and only accessible by air or sea. Pitt Island was exposed to the coastal island snow belt and cold temperatures in the winter, and to have to go down and work there in the winter wasn't attractive to anyone.

I met with Norman to share my new revelations about how to get the guys to work safer, and I even tried to convince him that maybe I was better served back in Prince Rupert over the winter, writing policy and procedure for the company. He didn't seem too fond of that idea, probably because it wasn't his idea. So on January 6, 1995, I flew down to meet Norman, who went in a couple of days earlier to set up the camp for a bunch of us.

Chapter Twenty-Seven
Where the Nightmare Begins
— Devon Lake

We worked down at the Devon Lake camp for about three weeks. It was a pretty soft job. The company we had worked for to log this block was required by the forestry to leave as little an environmental impact as possible, so I worked with Norman and three other guys during the day to gather up tree debris from the lake and move it onto shore, then transport that debris with dump trucks down to the landing three miles away and pile it up for burning. It was easy work and we got paid really well. I found out once I was there that the reason we were chosen to do the work was because it paid well and we had earned the gravy job, so to speak.

When I think of the guys in that crew, it was pretty stacked. Along with Norman, there and my cousin Gord, who was a heavy-duty mechanic. There was also a really hard-working guy named Ambrose, and a couple of logging truck drivers.

We had this huge bonfire that burned around the clock to get rid of all the log debris. The idea of logging this block of timber was to have the area look better than when we arrived. That meant cleaning up every bit of trash, and ensuring that no spills or leaks were anywhere. They were casual days, though. The winter daylight at that time of year on the coast means you can only see with natural light from about 8 a.m. to 4 p.m. each day. So that was our work time. Pretty slack compared to what we would work in the summer.

I had great chats at night with Norman sitting around the kitchen table in his camps on this assignment. This particular camp was a large, flat barge that was about 150 feet long by fifty feet wide. All the housing units were on top of the barge. The barge also had a dining hall that could seat about twenty-five guys, a recreation room, and a large area for laundry, bathrooms, and showers. Usually, everyone shared a room on this camp, except for Norman, of course. Being the owner and president of a logging company did carry some privileges.

When the camp was running in full swing, there was a cook and bull cook and approximately twenty guys staying together. Usually things went pretty smoothly, considering there were twenty-five guys living together who had all different types of lives and were married or divorced or you can imagine the rest. Amazingly enough, there were very few conflicts in these camps. Guys were there to work and they did a pretty good job of that.

So when we had just five guys in the camp doing this work, it gave each and every one of us a lot of face time with the boss. Maybe too much, because all of the sudden we were sitting in the main kitchen at this table that seated twenty-five or so, and we started to put together action plans and schedules for the coming year. Without having asked a single one of us to put anything together, we were all working at night without extra pay trying to figure out how to make this company more productive and safe.

Norman was a pretty smart guy. He brought us down for a reason. We were all helping him plan out the next year together. He didn't have to pay us extra. We all started doing it because he was. There are lots of way to motivate, and his was to lead by example. We would see him at night going over things and we would just naturally start asking questions and all of the sudden we were involved.

On one of these nights near the end of January, we were tasked with planning the movement of this camp and all its assets for a move from Devon Lake to Drake Inlet, which was about thirty-five miles away. This would mean that we would have to load all the logging equipment we had down there at our present site and move it by way of barge along the coast islands further south to Drake Inlet.

We would have to load two logging trucks, one excavator, one dump truck, two pickups, one ambulance, two log loaders, and two containers of equipment onto the barge. Then, once that was all accomplished, we would have to take all the water lines, sewer lines, and camp docks out of anchor and lift them onto the deck of the barge. Then we would do the same with all non-essential watercraft and also lash the ten sets of boom sticks we had to the rear end of the barge and tow it all to Drake Inlet.

That was a lot of weight and a lot of equipment. This tow was going to be about twenty hours. As a team, we formulated how to go about putting the equipment on the barge and then setting up the boom sticks for the tow and so on. During our discussions, we decided that I would go with Norman and Gord, my cousin, from Devon to Drake on Feb 11. We figured it would take at least a day to lash everything correctly to the barge before beginning the tow. We all were to have various roles. Mine was to ensure the boom sticks were all lashed properly and that the docks were lifted out of the water and placed on top of the barge.

There were long discussions that late January night about whether the tow could be done in twenty hours, and then even more talk about the open water that we would have to pass across to get to the top end of Princess Royal Island. For about seven miles of the tow the tugboat would be exposed to open water from the Pacific, and at this time of year the conditions and seas were not always favorable to crossing that much ocean.

Chapter Twenty-Eight
Pre-job Planning

This was back in 1995, before the Internet was in widespread use and cell phones were useless on the outer BC coast. There was no signal, so the only way to communicate was with the old "auto-tell" phones. which essentially just worked on a two-way radio channel. I figured if we were going to be moving all this equipment by water, I should check the coast guard weather report and ensure that the weather would be favorable. The weather reports were only a best guess back in 1995. The weather changed frequently on the coast, and many times with very little warning. We were planning to do this move on or around February 10. It was January 31, and the weather report only gave reliable indications about three days out.

As we wrapped the work up on the environmental cleanup down in Devon Lake, we decided to hold off until we had a better understanding of when we would actually be making the move. We had planned for February 10, but that could change. We worked another week, and as wrapped up one job we picked up another small hand log sale. This was requested by the BC forestry. A hand log sale is a small stand of timber that is easily accessible either by water or land that the forestry asks companies to thin out so that the new generation of growth can take hold.

Trees eventually die, and when they die while on the stump they lose all the stumpage value. The idea is to log them while they are still worth something. This also gives the smaller trees in the area a chance to flourish. By removing the bigger and older trees, the younger ones get the chance to grow into valuable wood.

We logged this small stand of trees and looked to be set for a

February 11 departure to Drake Inlet. We went over the details of the plan again as a group. Our version of a pre-job safety meeting. I took notes on who was to do what. We all had assignments, and as the meeting was drawing to a close, I thought I had better check the coast guard weather again. When I got the report, I came back to the meeting and asked Norman for a couple of minutes of his time.

He looked at me, puzzled, and asked the other seven guys to wait a minute. Norman and I went into a different room and scoured over the weather report. It was February 10, and the idea was to go the next day, but the weather report warned that a storm was brewing out in the Pacific and that it was expected to make the coast in the next five to seven days.

Norman stared at the paper with my notes on it. He asked me some very detailed questions about what else the report might have said. My answer was for us to go and listen to it together on the coast guard weather channel. We did, and Norman listened very intently. His eyes stared at the floor with great focus as he absorbed each word across the radio.

After listening to the report for a few minutes, he turned the volume down a bit and asked me what I thought. My gut was telling me to hold off, but that could be viewed as a sign of weakness in this get-r-done world. So I sat there and in milliseconds made a decision to expose my fears. I took the leap of cautiousness and said, "We may be gambling a little here." I had been seeing success in Norman's company lately with crews making choices that were safer, but to change Norman's behavior was a real challenge.

As Norman was still working through the scenario in his head, I was wondering about what was influencing his decision. Knowing the man as I did, I was sure he was debating internally the production and money cornerstones, not with the safety cornerstone, but against it. His actions continued to set the tone for the entire company. If he was still willing to gamble with safety, the guys would still gamble with safety.

Norman was still focused on the floor. His gaze signalled thought, deep thought. After a minute he took a deep breath and looked up at me and said, "We have a window of opportunity here. If we load everything up as planned tomorrow and we leave by 3 p.m., we will have ample time to get the equipment into Drake Inlet and we will still have three days to burn before the storm arrives."

His logic seemed good, although it still seemed like a little too close for comfort. I was basing my worries and fears off of my limited experiences. Norman had twenty-five more years working in this environment than I did. It made sense to me that he would have a better grip on the timeframe required to get this done properly and safely. Even though I could see the logic in the thought process, I also had this pain in my stomach that I could not ignore, that little sensation we get when we have a bad feeling that maybe something isn't quite right. I had that gut feeling that we were taking too big a chance.

I fired back with, "Are you sure we should do this?" I recognized that he was prioritizing production again. Norman was not used to being second guessed, and I could tell that my comment garnered his full attention, because he turned to face me and his gaze was upon me. We were almost the same height and were looking directly into each other's eyes. I saw no anger in them, just that continued concern. He looked at me for what seemed like days, but it was only a few seconds.

Then he cracked a little smile and said this, which will be carved into my brain forever. "We are good to go, and I'll tell you why. I would never put my people, my company, or my reputation at stake. If I didn't think we were good to go, then we wouldn't!"

It made sense. After all, this was a man who made me an active player in his company's safety program as a way to get me understanding the risks I put myself in front of without thinking. He was thinking through the process of moving the equipment and the time window we had. I had questioned whether we should continue based on my limited experience, and he logically explained his thought process and it made sense. So even though I did not totally agree with him, I didn't think I should push further because he had so much knowledge in this type of work. He also did not just rush to his conclusion. Norman was thinking this through. His explanation of the time available and the time required for the task made perfectly logical sense. I couldn't rightly argue with him if he made sense.

Norman was also bang on with respects to "his people, his company, and his reputation." He was ultimately accountable for everyone's life, and he took that role seriously. I had voiced my concerns and he had respectfully voiced his back and he made sense. So we went back into the meeting with the rest of the crew and finalized the details of our action plan for the next day's move.

It was a good meeting. I had task assignments for everyone and we all knew our roles. The next day at 7 a.m. we would start all the work and get it wrapped up.

I have to say this, too. I don't think I have ever seen pre-job work get done as efficiently as I did that day. There is an old saying, "If you fail to plan, you plan to fail," and we weren't going to be guilty of that on this job. We went over every detail and it was set out who would be doing what tasks the following morning. We went to bed that knowing we had our work cut out for us. We were ready.

When the next day arrived, we all had breakfast together—me, Norman, my cousin Gord, Ambrose, Corey, and our camp cook. The plan was to start the work at 7 a.m., and if everything went as planned, we would be done around 4:30 in the afternoon. We would then wait until 7 that night to tow the camp barge and equipment with the outgoing tide to get an extra push toward Princess Royal Island. As the tide turned inward, we would use that ocean current to our favor and propel ourselves toward the inner channel of Drake Inlet.

We would all go together on the tow and then set the camp up the next day against some pilings and all fly out together on a floatplane so that we could get some work done in town while the storm blew over. If the timing of everything worked properly, we would all be safe in Prince Rupert with a few days to burn before the storm came ashore. It was preplanning at its best.

Chapter Twenty-Nine
February 11, 1995

As February 11 progressed along, I could tell before even midday that we were well ahead of schedule. So much so, in fact, that when lunch came that day Norman changed the plans a little to accommodate our speed. His new idea was to have me take Corey and Ambrose and the camp cook back to town in the high-speed boat called the R Kaien, which was a very fast double hulled aluminum boat that could easily do speeds of forty miles per hour. Norman would then take the Kaien Pride tugboat with our mechanic, Gord, and do the tow a little earlier than planned.

It seemed pretty good to me. Norman figured if he and Gord got started out earlier, they would be able to fasten the barge and equipment to the piling at the end of Drake Inlet before noon, and then I could send a plane down to get them the next day. They'd all be back in town by early afternoon. It was planned that I would leave around 2 p.m. from Devon Lake, and if all went well, I would be back in Prince Rupert by about 4:30 p.m.

As we worked to that end it all came together beautifully. We were all ready just before 2 p.m. and the entire crew shared a coffee together. Then I began my departure with the other crew in the R Kaien high-speed boat. As I loaded gear into the R Kaien, I noticed Norman had a look in his eyes I had not seen before. It was a look of confusion.

He was following me around the camp. As I gathered my gear, he would walk behind me from one room to another as I grabbed my personal effects. Going home for a few days was unexpected, and I would use the opportunity to catch up on dirty laundry and buy myself some new winter gear. We weren't used to working in the months of February and March, and I was going to come back prepared.

As I moved from one room to another, I finally wanted to know why Norman was following me. It was a bit unnerving. He just smiled and said he was wondering if sending me to town with the other boys was the right thing to do. So we grabbed a last coffee before I set out, and he went over the route with me again. He reminded me to contact the marine traffic dispatcher on the R Kaien's two-way radio to let them know my route. That way if something went wrong, the coast guard could come and get us.

Because he showed so much concern on his face, I finally asked, "Would you rather we stay and go home tomorrow?"

Norman slowly brought his cup of coffee to his mouth and took a bite out of his Dad's cookie (a delicious brand of cookies), and said, "No, you guys will be alright."

I was just a little concerned with the wind as we headed toward Prince Rupert. The swells could build up and the waves might get a little high. High waves where I was from may be different than other places in the world. This was the west coast of British Columbia, where we were used to getting waves that were fifteen feet high or better. In fact, the Hecate Straights, which is an open channel of water between the Queen Charlotte Islands and the mainland, would commonly see storms that brought winds of one hundred miles per hour or more.

Even though the storm that was coming wouldn't be on land for several days, the waters ahead of that storm could be rough. The winds on this day as we were putting everything away for the tow were about thirty miles an hour. Inside the inlet, where we were protected from the wind, it was lightly blowing and the water had a mild, one-foot chop to it. So as Norman shared his concern, we decided that when I got out to the open water, which was about three miles away, I would radio Norman and let him know whether I would continue on or not. He would then decide based on that whether he should rethink his decision about moving the tow based on the information I provided.

The coast guard weather report showed that the storm was advancing faster than originally forecast. Instead of the storm making coastal waters on February 15 and 16, it was expected to arrive a day earlier, on February 14 and 15. Weather reporting is not yet a perfect science, but in the past fifteen years we have gotten much better at it. As an old friend of mine says, "I was a meteorologist, which meant I was a professional liar." Strange, but true. How many times has anyone planned an event when the weather looked great and then had to cancel that event because of weather?

So as we loaded our gear into the R-Kaien and pushed off from the dock at Devon Lake, Norman was still standing right there with his coffee cup. He looked at me and with great concern said, "Be careful. Do not take any chances. If the weather gets too rough, turn around and come back."

I yelled back, "No problem" as we started to pull away. The sound of the engine on our boat started to get louder as I increased the throttle. I looked back one last time—I was about 250 feet away from the barges and Norman was still standing on the dock, staring at us. As we roared away, he watched us as we got further and further away. I am willing to bet he kept watching us until he couldn't make us out anymore. I had a funny feeling in my stomach as I sped away in the R-Kaien. Sometimes we get these feelings in our stomach when we feel danger or that things are going to go badly. I had one now, and it scared me.

Chapter Thirty
Sick Feeling

Once I got out into the open water, it didn't take long to see that there were much bigger waves out here than in the protected inlet. We went about another mile before radioing Norman on the Kaien Pride tug. I was to ascertain whether I could make it to Prince Rupert almost a hundred miles away in this weather, and also whether the oncoming storm was moving toward the coast faster than reported. I needed to decide if I felt it would be safe for Norman to continue on with the tow to Drake Inlet.

As the water got rougher and rougher and the waves got bigger and bigger, we began to crash through the rolling waves at about two-thirds speed (twenty-five miles an hour), and we were getting some pretty good air. The R-Kaien was designed for this type of weather and sea condition. The hull of the boat was actually designed to push water away and out as the boat would either crash into or over the waves. So it was a very sturdy sea craft for only being twenty-three feet long. It was time for Norman and I to go over the decision on the radio. We began to talk, and I described the seas to him—the size of the waves, the direction of the wind, and so on. We spoke for a few minutes and then he asked this final question, "Do you think the Kaien Pride can handle the weather?" The Kaien Pride was a sturdy tugboat. She had been in numerous storms and ugly weather and had always come through with flying colors.

As the wind whipped the crashing water up around us and the sea spray blew over the windshield of the R-Kaien, I thought about how many times I had been on the Kaien Pride in less than favorable weather. There had been occasions when the Kaien Pride had found itself in much rougher seas than this and made it without trouble. The waves weren't really all that high, maybe seven or eight feet at this point. I was travelling in a much smaller and lighter boat, and the Kaien Pride had half its tonnage under water, which made it very sturdy.

Tugboats are designed to work in poor weather. A vessel like the Kaien Pride was about forty feet long, almost twenty feet wide, and drafted at least eight feet underwater. This meant that a lot of the boat was under the water line, and most of the boat's weight was in the engine and shafts so these tow boats had a very low center of gravity. This made them incredibly stable in rough seas.

As I talked with Norman back and forth on the two-way radio, I could see that on the horizon the water looked calmer than where I currently was. I told Norman to hang on about two minutes and I would call him back. As I travelled another half mile, the waves began to subside and the seas rolled and pitched much less. The wind was even dying down a few miles per hour because less water was being whipped off the wave tops.

It seemed to me at the time that the weather was worse right at the exit of the Inlet. I was travelling a different route than Norman was going to take, exactly opposite, actually. He was going to be heading southeast upon exiting the Inlet, and I was heading northwest around the outside of Pitt Island to Augdon Channel, and then up to Prince Rupert. So I tried to look as far south as I could to ascertain whether Norman's route would be faced with more or less intense weather.

Have you ever shared a comment or made a statement in your life and wished you could have it back? I grabbed the radiophone and called to Norman on the Kaien Pride and told him that the weather and seas looked acceptable down the coast on his planned journey. As I finished that statement on the radio, I again noticed that ugly feeling coming from my stomach. At this point I thought it was just nerves for having to take the boys home for the next two hours or so in these conditions. Either way I was feeling uneasy about the entire day.

Norman and I finished our communications, and he decided to head to Drake Inlet in a few hours. I traveled to Prince Rupert with the rest of the crew and we got in just before darkness set in at around 5 p.m. It was a cold ride home in the R-Kaien. The weather reports indicated that outflow winds from the Arctic would be picking up with intensity as the day drew on and that minus temperatures would follow.

Chapter Thirty-One
A Late Night Phone Call

I was glad when we secured the R-Kaien to the dock at the fuel station and got back to my apartment. I took a long, hot shower to get the cold out of my bones and then sat down with my fiancé and we had a late supper. I was telling her of the work plans for the next few weeks and we went over some of our wedding plans. We were to be married on July 25, 1995. We were bickering over the number of groomsmen and bridesmaids that we would be having and settled that dispute by watching a movie on TV.

I had fallen asleep on the couch somewhere between 10 and 10:30 p.m., and was awoken by the sound of the telephone. Nobody called me this late, so it had to be for my fiancé. I asked her to get it, so she wearily got up and answered the phone. She kept saying, "Hello? Hello? Hello?" and then she finally handed the phone to me and said, "I think it's for you."

When I placed the phone to my ear, all I could hear at first was a loud, whispering noise. It sounded almost scratchy. There was finally a small break in the squealing and I could make out Norman's voice. I could hardly make him out. He kept saying, "Can you hear me?"

My response was, "Kind of." This went on for several minutes while we talked on the phone. He was phoning me on the autotel phone from the Kaien Pride, so it was really scratchy and difficult to make out.

What I could get from our conversation was that Norman and Gord were held up in a bay about five miles from the end of Drake Inlet. They had made good time, but the reason they did was because they had gotten a big push from the winds and seas that were accompanying the storm, which had come faster than forecast and was now right on top of them.

That scratchy sound I kept hearing during our struggled conversation was the sound of wind blowing past the windows of the Kaien Pride as it was tied up in a bay. The reason Norman had tied the boat and the barges up where he did was because the storm was knocking the hell out of them. Norman told me that the wave swells were at least thirty feet high out in Prince Royal Passage, which was just down from the turn into Drake Inlet. They had made it into the bay and the mountains were protecting the water and the barge and tug from the storm's onslaught.

In the conversation I had with Norman, he told me that twenty-five feet or so above the water the winds were gusting to one hundred miles an hour, but that on the water twenty-five feet lower it was almost perfectly calm. The mountains in the bay were shielding the water from the waves and winds. There were minimal waves at sea level, and so being tied up in this bay was the best thing to do.

Norman went on to tell me that on the way through Princess Royal Passage the waves and wind had picked up so badly that the barge had some of its shacks blown off. We had built work rooms and a mechanical shop on top of the barge and drilled the structure to the steel floor of the barge, and they were thrown over the side like paper in the storm. Norm went on to tell me that when the waves were hitting the bow (front) of the Kaien Pride, that the waves would break and then go right over the top of the Kaien Pride's high bridge, which was a distance of about fifty feet.

Some of the docks that we had lashed to the side of the camp barge were broken apart and smashed to bits, and one skiff (a little fourteen-foot work boat) that was on top of the docks and also lashed down was missing and presumed sunk. All of this talk about what they had seen was scaring me. They were still down there and the storm wasn't showing any signs of letting up.

Norman also went on to share that he had tied a two-inch-wide by 150-foot-long rope around a tree onshore in the bay they were held up in. In Norman's words, he explained how he had tied the rope around a tree that had been on this mountain since Jesus walked the earth. Please remember this is the coast of Northern British Columbia, and some trees here are ten feet around or more. Norman had picked out the sturdiest tree he could and tied the Kaien Pride to that tree. The barge was still hanging off the stern (back) of the Kaien Pride.

The wind and ocean current were keeping the barge straight off the back of the Kaien Pride and except for the top of the tug and barge, everything was safe in this bay. The wind was only hitting the top bridge and mast of the Kaien Pride and roof of the barge. As long as nothing changed, they would ride the storm out here.

My heart was in mouth as Norman described all this to me. I had made the call earlier in the day to go ahead and perform the work. That decision didn't sit well with me when I made it hours earlier, and it was sitting even worse with me as I sat in the comfort of my living room while Norman and Gord were down there getting pounded in a storm.

I asked what they were going to do, and Norman came back with, "Nothing. We are going to sit right here and wait for this storm to blow itself out." The coast guard weather report indicated that the storm would pass over by midday, but that report had already been very wrong. Norman must have sensed my concern because he told me they would be okay. I'll never forget this line, "As long as we stay here we will be fine." I wanted to be assured that he was going to stay there in the protected bay, and he said, "We aren't going anywhere until this blows over."

Chapter Thirty-Two
Luck—When Does it Run Out?

"We got lucky," was how Norman ended the phone call. There was that word again. We used that word far too often. Anytime we did something and someone narrowly missed getting injured, we all would say it, "We got lucky." How many times would luck be on our side? This night it sure seemed it was. If Norman had left the inlet an hour later than when he did, he would not have made it into the Drake Inlet and would not have gotten into the protected bay.

Norman had described to me how as each minute went by the storm got worse and worse. The waves got higher and the wind got stronger. It was completely dark as he tried to navigate into Drake Inlet around midnight, and because the seas were so rough and the wind so bad, the radar, Norman's only real vision, was performing poorly. Whether it was all the wind or due to the rotation being thrown off by the rising and falling ocean swells, the readings were off and images would come and go.

Luck, as it were, was probably on our side that night. I have mentioned several times throughout these recollections that luck comes in two forms, good and bad. The funny thing about luck is that sometimes we think we were lucky and maybe we were actually unlucky.

Norman and I finished the conversation with him saying he would call me in the morning and let me know how or if they had moved and what the weather was doing. I sat on the couch in my living room and was describing to my fiancé the conversation I had just had and how sick I felt about it. We decided to move to the bedroom and call it a night. As I lay in the darkness of our bedroom, all I could think about was how close we had come to losing Norman and Gord. I sat there thinking about that for about an hour, and then I finally drifted off to sleep.

Chapter Thirty-Three
An Early Morning Phone Call

It was early the next day when the phone woke me up. We had an answering machine, but no one ever called me this early, so I thought it best to answer it. As I lazily reached toward the nightstand, it all of the sudden came back to me in an instant the last call I had received the night before. I grasped the phone and brought it to my ear, and I fully expected to hear that same scratching sound I had heard the night before, but the only sound I heard coming from the other end of the line was that of a woman who was very upset.

As I said hello, and after a long moment a lady spoke with a crack in her voice, "Dwayne, is that you?" It was Linda, Norman's wife.

"Yes," I said.

Again in a cracked voice she said, "Have you heard from Norman today?" I had not heard from Norman since last night, and because it was still dark, I thought it best to check the alarm clock. It read 7:13 a.m..

Now that I knew the time, I said, "No, I haven't talked to him today, why?"

Linda was silent for a few seconds and her voice cracked again as she said, "Gordie called me asking if I had heard from Norman."

I had gotten a phone call that same morning at 5:15, and when I picked up the phone there was no answer on the other end, just static. I asked repeatedly for someone to answer but no one did and after a few fruitless minutes of listening for nothing I hung the phone up and went back to sleep. So as I went through in my brain how the night had played out, I started to come to some pretty serious revelations.

It is amazing how many milliseconds it takes for our brain to assess data. Within those milliseconds I realized that something was very wrong. Gordie was with Norman down on the tow. For Gordie to be calling meant that something had happened and Gordie did not know where Norman was. Just as I was going to ask Linda what Gordie said he could see, Linda broke the silence with this, "Gordie called me from the phone on the camp barge and said he is floating around in the storm and the Kaien Pride is underwater and he could not see Norman."

Linda was crying as she finished that last part. As I sat there in the darkness, I began to realize the worst was unfolding in front of me. I was on the phone with the wife of the man who I had worked for and respected since I was first hired by them as a summer student almost eight years ago. She was crying, and there was nothing I could say to comfort her. As terrible as I felt, what must Linda have been feeling?

There were still many unanswered questions—so much to find out—but I was starting to feel that this was not going to be a good day. All indications were that Linda's husband and the father of their three boys was dead.

Her voice cracking again, she asked, "What should I do?" I told her I would call Gordie and be right over. I said I would be there as quick as possible to help find out what was going on. I was thinking the worst as I hung up the phone. I sat on the edge of my bed, and my head was racing a million miles an hour. My fiancé woke up. She looked at me confused and asked, "What is wrong?"

I tried to summon my strength. My answer back was, "I think Norman has drowned."

Chapter Thirty-Four
Has My Luck Run Out?

I phoned the camp barge from my home phone. It rang for several minutes, and then finally Gordie picked up. I had never heard him sound so unemotional. With a flat, monotone voice he could only mutter, "He's gone."

What did that mean? "Gordie, I need you to tell me more," was my response.

There was a long pause of fifteen seconds at least, and I could hear Gordie trying to control himself. He was whimpering like a small child. "He is gone ... I can't find him. The Pride was on its side and then underwater for a bit and when it came back up he wasn't on it."

So many questions flooded my head to ask Gordie. I asked, "Are you okay, where are you?" Gordie took a few seconds and said he was against the shore on the barge and that he was safe. He was trying to get a skiff (small fifteen-foot work boat) into the water off the barge to go look for Norman. "How long has it been since you saw him?" was all I could ask back.

Gord told me at least an hour, and that's when my eyes filled with tears. Because I had been phoned just minutes ago, I thought this event might have been unfolding right now. I had thought that mere minutes had passed, and that if I provided guidance I could help find Norman and get him to safety. Reality hits us hard sometimes, and it just tore right through my heart at 7:19 a.m. on February 12, 1995.

I couldn't hide my tears from Gordie anymore, and nor could he from me. We were 125 miles apart holding onto telephones, and I was crying. I could tell he already had been crying. I asked Gordie if there was any way he could be wrong. This is a natural human tendency to deny the truth in front of us. Sadly, all Gord could muster through a tearful voice was, "No."

We sat in silence for almost a minute until Gord asked if I was still there, and I answered with, "Yes."

Gord told me how he was going to try to tie the barge and equipment up safely and then see if he could get to the Kaien Pride as it was drifting lifelessly out in the bay. My only comment to Gordie was to not do anything that would put him in jeopardy and that I would be down right away. Gord's voice was still cracking as he said, "How the hell are you going to get down here? It is still blowing like a son of a bitch" I told him I would get there, just to hang on.

As I dressed and got ready to leave my house to go to Linda and Norman's, I phoned the coast guard and told them what was going on. They already knew. Gordie had been asking for assistance for over an hour. They had dispatched a coast guard vessel to the area and told me that a buffalo aircraft was also flying up from Vancouver Island to assist. Vancouver Island was about three hundred miles from Drake Inlet. Why would they send an aircraft from there? The local coast guard base also had a Sikorsky S-61 helicopter that they used for ocean rescues, and I figured that aircraft would also be heading down as well. If that were the case, then I wanted onto that aircraft to help in the search efforts.

When I asked over the phone if I could go down on the helicopter, the coast guard guy on the other end of the phone asked me if I was mentally challenged. He told me they wouldn't fly low-level flights in this weather, it was too risky. Again, the heaviness of the situation had eluded me as I was emotionally charged and not thinking rationally. This weather was still too bad for even the coast guard to fly in. So I did something that I don't regret but would hope that I have the foresight to never do again. I called in a favor from a friend.

As I mentioned earlier, I had worked in helicopter logging operations and had met a few people who still flew in the area. I phoned one of them to see if they would fly me down. When I called the base number it went to my friend on call, and I explained my situation to her and where I stood with the coast guard. I am not sure what I said to her, but she said to meet her down at the base in twenty minutes and we'd give it a try.

I don't want to give the impression that the coast guard wasn't willing to help. I have the highest respect for the people who work in those organizations. The men and women who put themselves at risk far too often because of someone else's circumstances are too many to count. The coast guard pilots that day were doing the right thing. They realized that if they went into that terrible wind and weather that they could be adding to the human toll. I want to make this clear—I hold no ill will whatsoever to the people who made the right decision *not* to fly that day.

I stopped at Linda and Norman's house and spoke to Linda for a few minutes. She looked terrible. I don't mean without makeup and hair done, but I mean she looked like she had aged twenty years in an hour. I met her and told her I was flying down to Drake Inlet to help out. I kept from Linda that Gordie had told me he had been gone for over an hour. That seemed insignificant right now. I was still hopeful that we would find Norman on a rock, cold and wet and swearing like a sailor. I hoped that Gord had just missed him. I was clinging to a small shred of hope.

Linda had tears in her eyes as I walked away to get to the airbase. I met her son, Jason, at the bottom door of the house. He looked so scared. He was twenty-one years old. He also looked as though he had been crying. He asked only one thing of me as I left the house, "Bring my dad home, Dwayne." As we locked eyes for several seconds he finished it off with, "Please." Then he lowered his head because he did not want me to see him cry. I reached over and grabbed him and hugged him tight. I said I would try, and as I wiped tears away from my eyes I walked out the back door.

Chapter Thirty-Five
All Hell Swirling Around Me

We flew from the airbase in a Bell 206, a small, incredibly versatile helicopter. It took only seconds once in the air to recognize how truly terrible the winds were. We were getting knocked around pretty good as we headed south. I remember thinking that the pilot, Andrea, and I could be victims two and three on this day.

In Prince Rupert it was very windy, but it was sunny. There wasn't a cloud in the sky. The winds that were causing us to get bucked around so badly were arctic outflow winds. This meant the temperature had dropped to well below freezing, and the winds were gusting to sixty-five miles per hour. We lifted off from the Seal Cove airbase at 8:30 a.m., and it was going to be rough ride down. I knew the route well, as I had been flying it or taking boats down Grenville Channel since I was about sixteen years old.

The storm was blowing itself out up near Prince Rupert, but as we flew each mile toward Drake Inlet, the winds would intensify. Although the sky was clear as far as I could see down toward Drake, and could tell that there were still some clouds. It was very dark down toward Drake, and as the seas opened up at the north end of Gil Island, I could see huge sea rolling waves out in the middle of the pass. I don't mean the fifteen to thirty foot kind, either, but huge, white-capped rolling waves that were more like thirty to forty-five feet high.

About ten miles from Drake Inlet, I could see a large ship crashing through the waves in the distance. This large sea vessel was getting pitched around as if it were a toy. Waves were crashing into the bow of this vessel and the wind was washing the spray over the back of the 140-foot-long boat. As we neared the vessel and were flying about two thousand five hundred feet above it, I could now make out that it was one of the coast guard ships that was sent to help in the rescue.

My only thoughts were, "If this large ship is getting bucked around like a cork in a bathtub, then what did the Kaien Pride have to endure?" Seeing that ship get smashed around put a lot of things into perspective. Sometimes when we are working in an office, we forget that our people maybe out in terrible conditions trying to accomplish their work. Sitting in the warm confines of an office miles from reality, we may wonder aloud why our crews aren't getting jobs done on schedule. To see that ship in these rough seas put it all in proper perspective. I could now understand why Gordie and Norman were in so much trouble and why also Norman was missing.

We flew past the coast guard vessel and made our way into Drake Inlet. My thoughts kept returning to Norman. Was there a chance that he was alive? Was he just in a spot where Gordie had not thought to look, and was cold and waiting for our pickup? I had not talked to Gordie for almost one and a half hours, as there was no way to communicate with him while we flew down. Was Gord okay? He was in the middle of hell. What would I see when I got down there?

As the helicopter started descending toward the narrow pass that is the entrance to Drake Inlet, I could see the Kaien Pride about two miles down the channel, upright and moving under engine power. This was a good sign to me, as the last communication with Gord had indicated that the Pride was floating around the storm without anyone at the helm. I could see small, thin puffs of black exhaust coming from the Kaien Pride's exhaust stack. It could only be two things. Either Norman was at the wheel of the tug, or it was Gord. Based on the position of the camp barge being tied now to the north side of the bay, I was hoping it was Norman.

Andrea told me over the headset to hang on. We were descending toward the Pride, and although the winds were less of a concern a few minutes ago at higher elevation, they were picking up again and buffeting the helicopter around as we dropped altitude. As we continued our descent Andrea, asked where I wanted her to go. There was no landing pad down here, so I pointed toward the Pride. Andrea and I had hardly said a word to each other during the one-hour flight down to Drake Inlet. She told me later that she was asking me lots of questions, but that I didn't answer any of them. I don't remember her asking a single one. My brain had obviously been thinking other thoughts.

I was afraid to speak. I had been holding back vomit and tears for over an hour now, and all I could muster was to point to the Kaien Pride. The tug was in the center of the bay, and as Andrea lowered the helicopter to about one hundred feet off the water and about fifty feet behind the tug, I knew the person inside the Pride would hear the whoop, whoop, whoop of the rotor blades. A figure emerged from the back door of the Kaien Pride. I stared intently as the figure came through the back door. I was praying it was going to be Norman ... please be Norman ... please be Norman ... god, please let it be Norman.

Chapter Thirty-Six
The Worst Afternoon Imaginable

I could tell even from one hundred feet away that Gord had been crying. As we hovered, suspended in midair, I looked again at the wheelhouse of the Kaien Pride to see if someone else was going to come out behind Gord. I realized that wasn't going to happen, and I hung my head and started to tremble. Norman was gone. No one needed to say it to me. The knowledge of what had gone on that day from what I was told earlier, and the sight of a coast guard boat getting pounded by massive, unforgiving waves brought a crashing reality to me. All I could do was hold my head in my hands and use every ounce of energy to keep my wits about me.

Andrea landed the helicopter on the wind-protected side of the bay. Based on wind direction and the fact that there was no wind on this side of the bay, I knew that we were very near where Norman had tied the Kaien Pride to the trees along the shoreline maybe six or seven hours ago. Andrea powered down the helicopter and I got out, trying to wipe the tears from my eyes. Gordie was coming close to shore in the Kaien Pride. The blades of the helicopter stopped turning and I walked over to a rock point to talk with Gord.

We got together and were both putting on brave faces and discussed whether Norman could have made it or not. Gordie lowered his eyes and said I should see something. What was he going to show me? My first fear was that he had the body inside the Pride. He turned back toward the boat, walked into the wheelhouse, and said, "Look at this mess—there is no way he could have survived." I sat in awe looking over the wheelhouse of the Kaien Pride. Everything on the inside of the boat was smashed. Oceangoing tugboats are designed with everything to be secured to walls so that nothing breaks away in bad weather. All cabinets have special locks on them that won't open unless pushed a certain way.

There were smashed dishes, maps, and charts. The fridge was torn off the wall and floor mounts, the captain's chair was broken in half, the fire extinguisher had broken free of its mounts, and there was water everywhere. Water was still dripping from the ceiling, the walls, and the floor. Several windows were cracked and a few had small holes in them. The telephone and radiophones were hanging loosely from screws that were also torn up badly. Whatever Norman had been going through in the Kaien Pride, if he managed to end up in the water, there was no way he could have lived.

Gordie and I sadly and sullenly decided he should get back into the helicopter and I would stay in the Pride. We painfully spent the rest of the day until almost dark looking for the body of Norman James.

We spent several hours going over the beaches and water and never did find Norman's body. I remember it being about 1 p.m. when a smaller vessel from the large coast guard boat we had passed on our flight down arrived in Drake Inlet. There were three coast guard crew in the smaller boat and they helped us search. At 3 p.m. our helicopter pilot, Andrea, notified me that we had to get back to Prince Rupert. If we waited much longer we would lose sunlight and she would have to leave us there.

The coast guard guys told me they would keep looking until dark and then they would look again tomorrow. They would use the main ship that was anchored just out of our sight as their base of search and rescue, but here wasn't going to be a rescue. I was told that the chances of finding Norman's body were very small, and that they believed there to be zero chance of survival.

I was twenty three years old walking the beach in Drake Inlet that day. It was thirty-eight days shy of my twenty-fourth birthday. As the engine began to start on the helicopter, signalling it was time to go, a coast guard crew member handed me something he had found floating on the water. It was one of the Kaien Pride's life preservers. I was shaking as I reached out and grasped the life ring. Tears began to roll down my face and I struggled for my breath. As I looked up to the coast guard crew member, I noticed that he had a tear running down his cheek, too.

The flight back to Prince Rupert was a quiet one. Gordie sat in the front of the helicopter with Andrea, and I sat alone in the back three seats. I cried the entire flight home. Not just because of what had happened in Drake Inlet—my dear friend Norman was missing and presumed drowned—but a terrible realization had come to me as this tragic day unfolded. I was going to have to go to see Linda and tell her that her husband was dead. Say that word slowly out loud to yourself, "Dead."

There was no way I could ever tell Linda that Norman was dead without it being traumatic. I still wanted to tell her in a manner that would offer some sort of gentleness. As each minute passed by on the flight home I cried harder and harder. I would shortly be explaining to Linda that Norman was never coming home, and that I played a part in it. How on earth could I tell her how sorry I was?

The flight home from Drake was quick. The flight down in the morning seemed to take forever, but the flight home to Prince Rupert didn't last long enough. We made it home and Gordie and I got into my pickup truck. I started to drive him home, and he looked at me and asked, "How are you going to tell Linda?" He spoke so softly when he asked. It was as if he was even fearful to have to think of the coming conversation himself. I didn't even answer. More tears just ran down my face.

Gord asked me to drop him off at his father's house, because I had to pass by it on the way to Linda and Norman's. As I pulled into his father's driveway, Gord sat there with me in silence for five minutes. We looked at each other several times. Each time it looked as if he was going to speak, he just stopped and looked to the floor. There were no words. Finally, he looked at me as he clasped the handle to open the passenger door and moaned the words, "My god," and shook his head and got out of my truck.

I continued my dreaded drive to Linda's house.

Chapter Thirty-Seven
No Words

As I drove to Linda's house, I still hadn't figured out what I was going to say. I was so scared. There would be no perfect way to break the news. As I pulled into the driveway, I was surprised to see many vehicles parked in the driveway. This surprised me, but it shouldn't have. There are two types of news … good news and bad news. Bad travels fast. The bad news had travelled so fast that friends of the family had shown up to sit with, pray with, and hope with Linda that Norman would be found alive.

As I parked my vehicle, I realized that not just Linda was going to be getting this news at once … an entire town was. As I walked to the front door, I decided not to knock. I walked in quietly. Once inside the front door, I was surprised to see that no one was on this first floor. Everyone was upstairs on the main floor near the dining room and kitchen.

I could hear the people upstairs talking loudly, and although I couldn't make out any one conversation, I could hear that some people were crying and some were praying. I had to walk upstairs to get to the top floor. I walked the first eight steps to a small landing. I began to walk up the rest of the stairs when someone in the room saw me coming and let out a gasp.

When I heard the gasp I looked around and saw a few eyes were on me, but most were looking over to the top of the stairs. I looked up to the top of the stairs to see a very fragile-looking Linda standing there. She had just walked from the kitchen to meet me at the stairs. The room fell completely silent as I made my way up those last eight steps. Linda stood just off the top of the stairs to the left to allow me to get to the top. There was no way that I could hide the toll the day had taken on me. I had been crying most of the day, and my throat hurt from yelling out Norman's name as I walked the shoreline of Drake Inlet.

I didn't have to say anything. I got to the top of the stairs and walked to Linda, who already had tears running down her cheeks. I couldn't summon the courage to say he was gone. Linda had tears running down her face and her cheeks glowed red. She blurted out, "Where is he, Dwayne?" I couldn't bring myself to tell her he was gone. As more tears streamed down my face, I lifted my hands to the sides of my head and wrapped them around my neck. Linda lowered her head and started to cry. I had just crushed her. She began to weep loudly, and everyone in the house began to cry out loud.

Linda's son, Jason, stood right behind her, looking at me. His eyes started to swell, and then after a few seconds of trying to hold it in he started to cry as well. I looked back to Linda just to see her leaning toward me. She fell into my arms, crying. I put my arms around her and held her tight. She was shaking and crying.

Linda put her head into my chest and with both hands grabbed at my chest beside her face. She was crying so much. She kept her head buried in my chest while she asked this question that will haunt me forever, "What am I going to do?" I stood there with a grieving widow, a mother of three boys, and until a few hours ago, a wife to Norman. Her world had come to an end. The friends and family who had gathered throughout the day were all crying. An entire room of people, some strangers to each other, were holding hands, hugging, and pouring out their emotions.

I held Linda up. She was so weak. Jason was standing alone a few feet from us. He was just staring at the floor while tears fell from his face. He was standing alone. The shock of the day finally overtook him and he let it all out. I always thought in these situations that people would immediately grab for their loved ones, but both Jason and Linda were in such shock that they forgot who to grab.

Linda was still clutching me and Jason was alone, so I extended my hand to him and made a motion for him to join us. He slowly came over and put his arms around his mom and we stood there unabashedly remembering Norman. We stood there for a minute or so, and then Linda looked up at me while holding onto my chest and asked again, "What am I going to do, Dwayne?"

The tears streamed down her now reddened cheeks. I looked down to her, took her face on my hands, and quietly whispered to her as a tear fell from my face onto hers, "I don't know, Mom, I don't know what we are going to do without Dad," and then pulled my mother Linda Rae into my chest tightly and pulled my bother Jason even closer into us as the three of us stood at the top of the stairs in our house and wondered how we were going to live without our father and husband, Norman James Rae.

Chapter Thirty-Eight
Remembering Norman

Norman James Rae died on February 12, 1995 at approx 5:15 a.m. in Drake Inlet on the coast of British Columbia when he rolled the dice one too many times and put himself and others in a situation where they all could have died. My cousin Gord was with my father when the tugboat Kaien Pride was washed under the water while caught in arctic outflow winds during a storm. Thank god that my dad had decided to leave Gord on the barge while he towed the camp barge around the horn of Drake Inlet or there would have been two deaths for sure.

Ironically, I was supposed to be on the tow with dad from Devon Lake to Drake Inlet. If I had been with my dad as planned, I would not be here to write of the tragedy. Someone else would have written about two or three deaths. Or maybe there wouldn't have been an incident at all?

It was my father, Norman, who came to me while I was lying in a hospital bed all banged up from being in the avalanche and declared that he wasn't going to let me kill myself while I worked for the family business. He was willing to let me go and fire me, because, as he put it, "I am not going to have your death on my shoulders, Dwayne."

My father was good at lots of things. He was a good friend to those who he befriended, he was a good man to those whom cared to know, he was a terrible hockey goalie, as proven at old timer after old timer tournament, he was a pretty good business man, he was trusting to a fault, but what Norman was great at was being a father and husband. I have friends who all have fantastic parents, and they all love their parents dearly, but when I went to my twenty-year reunion, I had friends in their late thirties come up to me with tears in their eyes telling me how much my dad meant to them. Fifteen years later and the respect for dad still pours in.

Chapter Thirty-Nine
Aftermath

When Dad died that February day, our youngest brother Daryl was attending Notre Dame Academy in Wilcox, Saskatchewan, a private school some three thousand kilometers (about eighteen hundred miles) from Prince Rupert. Within minutes of realizing the tragedy of dad's death we had to figure out how to get either Jason or myself to Wilcox overnight so that our youngest brother would not find out over the phone or on TV that our father had drowned.

Jason and I talked quickly and we decided that he should go and I would stay with Mom and deal with the world falling apart. I don't know how Jason summoned the courage to do it, but he was on an airplane within one hour of finding out Dad was gone. He made it to Regina, rented a car, and drove to Wilcox and broke the news to Daryl at approximately 2 p.m. on February 13.

Daryl's big attraction for going to the Notre Dame Academy was his passion for hockey. Daryl was a good young hockey goalie and Notre Dame was Canada's version of our hockey universe. I can't imagine how Daryl felt when Jason broke the news to him. Daryl was mom and Dad's baby. They had decided after Jason and I that they had enough children, but five years after Jay's birth, Mom and Dad decided to give it another try and along came Daryl. Daryl was innocent compared to Jay and I. He was full of curiosity. He would ride around with dad and ask a million questions about why this and why that. That must have been fun for Dad, because Daryl was always with him.

Daryl was sixteen when dad died. When I was sixteen I was worried about the color of my Triumph sports car and whether I was going to lose my virginity. When Daryl was sixteen he lost his father.

Daryl's team pictures were scheduled the afternoon that Jason broke the news to him. I don't where he got the courage to do it, but Daryl had his team photos done with his teammates. Jason was at his side, holding him, comforting him, and once Daryl's teammates learned that he had just lost his dad, they all came over and offered support, love, and friendship.

Once the team pictures were done and Daryl's teammates finally allowed him to go, my brothers drove to the airport in Regina and boarded a plane to fly back to our tragedy.

The next day—Valentine's Day—was twenty-seven years to the day that mom and dad had their first date. I met Daryl at the airport, but he didn't say much until we got home. In the family room of our parent's home he broke down and fell into my arms and cried so much he fell asleep.

We lived in a catatonic state for weeks. Part of you wants to scream out as loud as possible, which is something I did on the day Dad died down in Drake Inlet. I had a very loud, angry conversation with God on the back of the Kaien Pride that day. Through teary eyes I let out a lot of anger, wrongly. I had prayed for many years to God to keep my father safe. I knew that the risks my dad took could mean that he would be dead too young.

When the unimaginable reality started to hit me down in Drake Inlet, I blamed God. I don't know why. Probably because God, in whatever form, couldn't argue back. Also maybe because I blamed myself and it just seemed easier to look outside and blame than inside and accept responsibility.

I was angry. In truth I was angry for years afterward. My father offered me a personal peace within myself while he was alive. Dad allowed me to be confident in who I was. I never felt judged, and he reminded me when I was crossing the line of confidence over to arrogance. When Dad died I tried to hide my guilt, and anytime anyone questioned me on anything, I would respond in a very immature fashion. It was my shield against the saber, so to speak. In retrospect, it was probably my saber against another saber—my way of extinguishing or masking my guilt.

For years our father had taken chances that no sane person would take. He had managed to break parts of his body, or in some cases tear them open and one part almost rotted off. Dad took so many unnecessary chances. We all laughed and said he had nine lives with a laugh. Mom reminds us today that she didn't laugh much in the months leading up to Dad's death, because she knew his luck was going to run out.

When I was leaving Mom and Dad's house to look for Dad the day he died, I met Jason at the door of our parent's home. Jason and I had trouble seeing eye to eye for most of our lives. Call it what you will, but Jason and I were just too much alike and that can cause issues. Jason grabbed me at the door of our home and was shaking when he hugged me with teary eyes and asked me to bring Dad home. It is a defining moment of our lives. We were never so close as that moment. I had a terrible feeling in my stomach that Dad was gone, but I couldn't admit this to Jason. He looked so scared.

I remember saying to Jason that Dad was probably sitting on a rock somewhere, mad and cold and embarrassed. I remember as the words left my mouth that I did not really believe them. I don't think Jason did either.

I told him that I would bring Dad back, and I didn't. It took Jay and I many years to get to the point we are at today. We can talk again without anger, without agenda, and remember the man that our dad was, happily. Dad would have been proud in the end. His death tore us apart for many years, but as time went on we forgave. We learned to love, to pick up the pieces, and wait for the sun to rise again.

Chapter Forty
From the Brink

How do I start to explain a family's path from the brink? When we lost Dad, we lost our way. My father was the patriarch of the Rae family. Remember earlier when I mentioned a worker named Wilfred said in an argument with my dad that he wasn't going to let happen to him what Norman let happen to someone else? My father lost his dad in 1973. My grandfather died working up the Skeena river, right near Alder Creek. When my papa Bernie died, he drowned just like Dad, and my papa Bernie was working for my father at the time.

Try and imagine the sick irony in that. My dad lost his dad in a very similar fashion that I lost mine. This is all in the same family. It makes me sick to think of the choices that my dad made. He knew the consequence that could happen more than anyone. My father searched for his father, just as I did. My dad told me that he walked the banks of the Skeena River crying out his father's name, knowing he was gone, just as I did, but he kept calling out because he didn't want to believe his dad wouldn't answer.

When my papa Bernie died, my father became the glue for the family to rely on. Dad was married to mom for almost four years when Bernie drowned. I was two years old and Jason was just a baby. Papa died two weeks after Jason was born. My father told me once that he was furious with his dad three days before his dad drowned because Papa Bernie told my dad how proud of him he was, that he had a beautiful family, and that if Bernie was to die tomorrow he would do so happily because of the life he had with his children and grandchildren.

My father did not take this well, and he gave Papa Bernie shit for thinking it was okay to go. My dad had that exact conversation with me three days before he drowned. On February 9, 1995. My dad, knowing I knew of the talk he and his father had years earlier, shared with me how happy he was in his life. How much he loved mom, how proud he was of Jason, how Daryl was going to be a superstar as a goalie in hockey, and how he saw me taking over the reins of the family company and taking it in directions he couldn't.

Of course I was furious with him as well. I asked him what he was trying to prove. I reminded him I knew of his conversation with his dad, and the end result. I asked, "Are you going to just kick off, too?" I laughed it off, but a few weeks after dad died I remembered the conversation, and it hurt. Dad was proud of his boys and us of him,, and when our glue was gone there were some rough times emotionally.

I didn't sleep for weeks, and slept poorly for years. This trend continued on for nine long years. Finally, in 2004, I hit the wall. Every time I met someone I thought they knew I blamed myself for dad dying. Imagine thinking everyone you talk to thinks you are guilty for something you really shouldn't blame yourself for. Tremendous stress is a result.

When I say I hit a wall in 2004 I am not kidding. I started to break down mentally. I was used to being a sharp thinker, quick with answers and able to prioritize and remain focused. My lack of sleep for that long period took a mental and physical toll. I finally ended up very sick. I was off work for two months to get right again. I had to deal with something I had pushed into the basement for nine years. I had to start working on accepting that I didn't kill my father.

I had convinced myself that Dad was dead because of my inactions. I thought that if I had said more at the pre-job meeting on February 11, 1995, that he would be alive. I had to work through that reality. Dad made his choices. I tried to help him make the right one, but he still made the final choice. I know I could have asked questions that would have aided in my presentation of my case for him to not do the task, but he would have done what he wanted.

It took some time to heal. Some wounds are visible, like the scars from my tumble down a mountain. Those scars are still visible, others are not visible and they never heal over and they bleed emotion and fear. Those scars finally began to close nine years later. I am still healing from the aftermath. I wish my path was different, but I wouldn't be sharing what I know around the world if I hadn't ended up on the path I did.

I remember Debbie Shelley, the CEO of Global International, asking me while working together, "Dwayne you have an intensity that most people don't have. What is going on inside that head of yours?" I had known Debbie about four weeks at this point and was seriously considering leaving her organization. It is her company that I contract with today, travelling the world and sharing our passion around workplace leadership. I was thinking of leaving her company because the pain I felt. I was having trouble sleeping again, and I was fearful I was going to end up in a bad state like 2004.

I told Debbie that I was wondering what my father would think of what I was doing not utilizing his lifetime of teachings in logging. I was about ten seconds away from telling Debbie I was quitting my position, when she said, "Dwayne, your father would be extremely proud of what you do today. You are trying to save lives before they need saving. Any father would be proud of that."

Well done Debbie, its almost three years later and I travel the world speaking of leadership behaviors and how to influence change. I have a passion for safety leadership that I have been told is undeniable and infectious, and I look to my father and his experiences for inspiration.

Debbie summed up what I never heard my father say. I knew that Dad was proud of Jason and Daryl and me, but he came from a time when parents didn't heap praise on their children. I had worked hard to help with the family business and it wasn't all roses all the time.

Dad was an asshole and stubborn as a mule, traits I inherited, but he was also caring and playful. Maybe part of the reason I couldn't get over his death was due to unanswered questions.

I had never heard from Dad that he was proud of me. I was never told by Dad that he loved me. I know he did—he showed tremendous affection. Again, it wasn't his generation's way to tell their kids they loved them every time they talked. My mom summed it up perfectly a few years back. She said, "Your generation says they love their children, our generation showed them what love was."

That goes right back to either saying the right things, or doing the right things. Which one is more powerful?

Daryl struggled through Dad's death. For awhile I took on the role of older brother and tried to be his father as well. I tried to give guidance and support and probably got it wrong. It's amazing that Daryl is the great person he is. He and I sorted or roles out. We talked openly and he never made me feel judged.

Jason and I are a different story entirely. Jason and I were to similar growing up. Neither of us wanted to admit that, however. We both craved Dad's attention, and I would bet that I got more than Jason, and he was keeping track. He noted in his head when I got to spend more time with Dad growing up, who had Dad as a coach for hockey or baseball, and who got to work with Dad more.

This tally drove a wedge between Jason and me before we were even out of high school and we grew further apart once I was working with Dad fulltime. I liked to work the laborious jobs, Jason didn't seem too. I liked to get up early (when Dad was up), and Jason liked to sleep until noon. This added to the rift between us. I saw Jason as lazy, and Jason saw me as Dad's favorite. Dad didn't have favorites, he made that clear to both of us, but when you are convinced of something, it becomes reality.

Our relationship soured further when Jason came to work for Dad a few years after high school and he had me as his boss. That was the tipping point. He used to come to me a lot and tell me that the guys hated me. I used to tell him the guys thought he was lazy. I would rather be known as a hard ass than lazy. You can see our issue.

I was a hard ass, and Jason wasn't really lazy. He was just not built as I was for certain tasks physically, and his lack of experience in logging made me view him negatively. But I failed to provide him the coaching he needed to excel. I was the reason a lot of what was going on between us was happening.

So when Dad drowned and Jason realized that he wasn't going to get the opportunity to bond with dad the way he wanted, who do you think got the brunt of Jason's anger? It took Jason and I a long time to be able to speak openly and without fear of opening up a can of worms. The truth is, once Jason had kids with his beautiful second wife, Robin, he began to realize what I did years earlier when I had Zack and Bailey.

Family is everything. Dad was our glue, but he was long gone and we needed to find a new adhesive to keep us together. That adhesive was our children, we as adults recognized that we needed to let them experience each other and smile together at their wonderment.

In the end, through death, we are where we should be—together.

Chapter Forty-One
Pieces of a Puzzle

After dad's death, Mom was so scared that something bad was going to happen to her boys that she forbade Jason and I from working in logging. That was tough because it was all we knew. I didn't want to fly commercially anymore and my training in my young life had all been around learning how to manage a logging company, and it was the same for Jason. Daryl was still young enough that he could learn new skills.

About six months after February 12, 1995 a local health club closed its doors. Our little town didn't have a place for me to work out. I had spent years trying to build my body and without a health club in town it would make that difficult. Working out was a physical and emotional release for me. It provided me balance. It almost seemed a calling that I get involved in the fitness industry, so with little experience and next to no practical knowledge, I opened up a health club.

Too make a really long story short, don't open up a health club. I threw tens of thousands of dollars into a money losing venture. I gained invaluable experience in running the health club and even opened up a second later on, but that experience was costly.

I stayed away from logging for a short period of time. Mom eventually let me back into the industry and I consulted while I owned the health club for years. It was never the same once Dad was gone. I consulted to various companies for about four years until a businessman offered a joint venture opportunity that involved a hand logging operation and sawmill.

So while owning and operating a couple of health clubs separated by almost one hundred miles, I opened up a small sawmilling and logging operation. For a time I really enjoyed it. It was 1999, four years after Dad's death, and the industry kept wanting me back, so I kept going back.

It wasn't the same. I used to laugh a lot when Dad and I worked together. Problems in operations came up, we talked through them, figured them out, had a coffee, and moved onto the next decision. When I was making the decisions alone, I didn't have the experience I needed. I wanted Dad's, and he was gone. The result was uneducated decisions based on limited experience, and in the end, the market conditions got the best of me.

The collapse of the soft lumber market in 2000 and the Canadian and American disagreements over tariffs and trade resulted in my saw milled wood being worth half its original value almost overnight. Imagine being told that your operational worth was just adjusted from five million in inventory to about 2.5 million. That really puts it in perspective.

I had no choice but to close that chapter of my life and look to a different industry for a career. Ironically enough, the same market conditions that shut down my sawmill also did the same to several large sawmills and a pulp mill in the Prince Rupert area. The result was thousands of job losses. That was the final nail in the coffin for my health clubs as well. The resultant population departing the area and people having less disposable income meant I had to close the gyms I owned.

The vibrant area I grew up in, where opportunity seemed to abound, was disappearing. If you wish to see the aftermath of economic depression for a large region, go to the north coast of British Columbia.

Prince Rupert was no longer the land of opportunity, so I moved to northern Alberta. I found work with a drilling company, worked my way through the management ranks, and then decided a few years later to leave drilling and get into production. I was given really great opportunities by a friend and businessman named Trent Guest who started an energy service company and allowed me to put in place a safety program that required operations to be linked to the core message.

It was a gamble for a young entrepreneur like Trent, but our safety program won an award from Canada's largest energy company in 2005 for excellence in safety and operations. This was the springboard that I needed to push the "safety as a value, not a priority" agenda forward.

This was a huge lesson for me. No wonder I couldn't get an entire workforce to embrace working safely. If I wasn't completely committed, how could they be?

I left Trent's organization and expanded my horizons with a much larger, but dysfunctional, company. I built a production department that was a revenue monster. I worked for the organization for almost three years, and learned about different leadership styles. I saw wonderfully talented people who were not allowed to have a voice, and watched as they were openly disrespected. It didn't exactly make for an ideal working environment.

I made my feelings openly known about one leader in particular, and he decided it was time for me to go. No skin off my back. Anyone who leads by poor example and is dishonest is someone I didn't want to work for. I remember thinking that I might have been influenced too often by making profit at the expense of the health, safety, and environment of the special people who worked with me.

I was sitting at home a few days after my departure looking for some direction, when my phone rang and it was a friend of mine who wanted me to talk with him about leadership training. "What the hell is leadership training?" I asked. Troy explained to me that when he saw me work with my team, he noticed they were mesmerized when I spoke. I had no idea. Troy told me to think of how my office at work looked. I had an office that was about twenty by twenty, with leather couches. It was always full of people.

He told me, "Dwayne, when you talk, people want to listen." He said I had a great message around safety. So when Troy told me he wanted me to meet the owners of Global International and discuss leadership training, I was surprised, scared, and hesitant.

When I told my wife I was thinking of doing this work, she was surprised. She commented that I wasn't social enough. I listened and wondered and then decided to give it a shot by facilitating a couple of modules for Debbie Shelley, the CEO, Delor Silva, the president, and Bas Owel, who is now the vice president. What a train wreck. I am known throughout Global as "Don't do what Dwayne did."

I must admit, it was brutal. I had never done this before. I had very little guidance, coaching, or direction, and just got up in front of these people and made a mess. The first module took about sixty minutes. Then they all left the room and gave me a ten-minute break, and then let me try a module called incident management. That one went better, but not much.

Too make a long story short, Delor came back to the room and said that the Debbie and Bas were hesitant to allow me to work with Global. However, Delor wasn't, and he made a side bet with them to convince them I would be a good fit for the team. Delor reminds every so often that it was he was the one who got me in, which always makes everyone laugh.

I then learned the craft, watched some amazingly passionate people talk about safety leadership, and learned the required skills. I have spent the last two and a half years travelling the world and speaking to executives and managers about behavioral choices and how we influence them. Before this, I had never loved anything as much as I did logging when my dad was alive. I think I love what I do now even more than logging with dad. To have the pleasure of working with people and helping them on their personal journey toward safety has been tremendously rewarding.

Through my life experiences, I have influenced thousands of people to make their own choices to work safely. Dad's death has saved lives.

Chapter Forty-Two
A Final Letter

Daryl talks about you with me all the time. He asks lots of questions. He didn't get enough time with you. He looks so much like you (other than his bald head ... where did that come from?) He sounds like you, too. It is very strange, sometimes he says something when we are together and the hairs stand up on my neck. It's like hearing your voice.

Jason and I laugh fondly when recalling our times working with you. The holidays we used to take to California when we would drive you up the wall with our insecurities and immaturities. Like me, Jay tried to leave logging behind after your death. But he became a helicopter pilot and found himself heli-logging again, this time from the pilot's seat.

I still struggle with you being gone. We spent almost four straight years together when I came back from college to help with the family business. I think sometimes the reason Jay and I didn't see eye to eye is due to the time I got to spend with you. He was rightly jealous. You were fun to be around and I got the mother lode.

I talk about you around the world. I wonder about my role in speaking up more when we planned the tow from Devon to Drake Inlet. I should have spoken louder. Until recently, I carried much guilt over not speaking up. I had to forgive myself, Dad. It was so painful ... god. Tears are rolling down my cheeks right now—I guess it still is.

I saved the worst or best for last: Mom. She nearly died when I broke the news to her. We all watched her closely for a year after you died. She did not recover well at first. It took her a long while, but she came through with the class she always showed as we grew up. Mom remarried five years after you died. I got to walk her down the aisle.

That wasn't easy. I had to hand her off to a man who wasn't you, but a man who loves her, and she loves him. That's why it is okay. I remember a conversation you and I had when you said, "If something happens to me, support your mother in moving on."

Mom married a man who saved you from another accident. Remember the Sagra barge you were towing that flipped over? Well, Mike helped you beach that barge and somehow got it upright. You were such a risk taker. You were a jackass. I say that laughing … you took so many stupid chances. Why?

Mom will find this out now for the first time. You told me two days before you died that if anything ever happened to you, that I was to support Mom and do whatever I could to help her move on. She speaks of you often with laughter and occasional tears. I asked her last year, the day before my son Zack had serious spinal surgery in Vancouver, if she was happy. She broke into tears. Mom said she was very happy, but that nobody had asked her that for years. After you, died people asked it all the time, but after a year or so they stopped and she was surprised that it was me asking.

You now have seven grandchildren, and a couple of divorces in the family history. Jason and I both have had two kicks at the marriage can. I think the second wives for each of us will stick. I have a son, Cameron, who is from my wife Maria's first relationship. I have two kids from my first marriage: a daughter, Bailey, and a son, Zachery, whose middle name is Norman.

Jason is remarried and has two sons named Jack and Luke. Daryl is married with a daughter named Taylor and a boy named Jayden. I told mom when she and Mike got married that if she had kids at fifty, I would kill her, and him.

Jason and I share many funny stories. Most involve you swearing too much and the three boys fighting for your attention. We always knew what we had when you were alive, we just didn't realize how much we would miss it until you were gone.

We miss you, and we will always love you.

What if. I will wonder forever.

What if I could have convinced you to listen to me.

About the Author

In early 2008 an internationally recognized organization dedicated to safety leadership training around the world approached Dwayne Rae and asked him to try and facilitate a couple of modules from their safety leadership program.

The try out didn't go all that well, but the owners of the organization made a comment that Dwayne had the ability to be a rock star in the leadership business if he could harness his life's lesson and share them with participants.

Its almost three years later and Dwayne has travelled the world sharing his unique experiences and touching people in a way rarely seen. Whether it is the CEO of the world's largest companies that he works with or the hands on the tool worker, Dwayne connects with them all.

Having witnessed terrifying workplace incidents throughout his short 39 years. Dwayne selflessly shares his adventures in the workplace and asks others to look within themselves to understand if they have made similar choices.

Dwayne's willingness to share his personal tragedies shows a tremendous desire to ensure other don't learn the way he did.

The passion he writes with is clearly evident, Dwayne's recollections in this book have been described as horrifyingly beautiful.

This book is easy to pick up, but near impossible to put down.

If you are going to read this book or attend a session to hear Dwayne speak, be prepared to be moved emotionally and intellectually.

From this book, you will "want-to" ensure you always make the safe choice.